A Heart In Need
of Repentance

A Heart In Need of Repentance

Denise Tucker

To order additional copies of this book, contact:
Xlibris Corporation
1-888-795-4274
www.Xlibris.com
Orders@Xlibris.com
116001

Contents

Dedication

I dedicate this page to my sister Deborah Gray Walton and my brother Jemal Gray who is now resting in Jesus' arms. They both have gone home to be with the Lord. You two shall forever hold a special place in my heart.

Acknowledgments

I would like to acknowledge my lord and savior, Jesus Christ for His sacrifice on the cross so that His words would be heard through my voice. I also want to express my gratitude to my four children who has always been my inspiration, Larry, Terri, Donny and Tony. It is because of your love, patience, acts of kindness and faith that you have shown me and it has given me so many more reasons to be proud of you all. As you continue to grow in the Lord, give Him your all so that you will do greater exploits in Him. Don't ever quit. There is so much more in Him for you to get and to give to a dying world.

You all have had major life experiences as adults and have made it through with the Lord. I want to add to what you already know be strong in the Lord always by continuing to read his word. Remember to pray always keeping an open communication with Him. Trust in Him always and do not lean to your own understanding, acknowledge Him and allow Him to direct your paths. Finally, I expect you to pass this on to your children and your children's children and to anyone else who will listen. Love you much.

Mom

Introduction

BELIEVE IT OR NOT

The day you die is better than the day you are born.
(Ecclesiastes 7:1)

None of us can hold back our spirit from departing
None of us has the power to prevent the day of our death.
(Ecclesiastes 8:8)

I once heard of a man from Utah who had a choice to make: live or die. This was a man who lived life on the edge by climbing rocky mountain peaks. It's told that he peaked forty-five of them most after midnight and he loved the adventure during the winter. Unfortunately, while climbing off of one, some rocks shifted, trapping his right hand against the wall of a narrow crevice in a remote canyon. Unable to free his hand, he tried shoving the rock with his shoulder, which was futile. He then tried freeing himself from the boulder by taking a knife chiseling his way out. Neither was he successful when he attempted to hoist the boulder with his climbing rope and pulley. The boulder did not move. After being trapped for a number of days, no one heard his loud screams. All his food and water was gone, and he was feeling depressed, helpless, and hopeless. Unsuccessful at any attempts of freeing himself the young, adventurous, mountain climber had an idea. If he could cut his hand off from his arm, he could be set free. It was risky, but it was his only chance to escape. So he made a decision to free himself by severing his right hand.

The young man began by first breaking the bones in his wrist. Then with some kind of tool stored with his supplies, he proceeded to saw into his own skin. He could hear his bones cracking as he continued the amputation process When he finished, he proceeded to break free from the boulder. The man ran down the mountain back to civilization with one hand. Down the hill he met tourist who assisted him. The decision he made spared his life. Even though it meant living with one hand, the man's decision was to choose life over death.

Amazingly, the man set himself free from dying on the mountain that cold, wintery day. Nonetheless, there is a time that death will come to him again. Regrettably, however, he will not be able to escape or free himself from that appointed moment. In fact, there is a date when death will come for all of us and we will not be able to break away, break out, run, or hide. The Bible puts it this way, "None of us can hold back our spirit from departing. None of us has the power to prevent the day of our death" (Ecclesiastes 8:8). You may feel it is morbid to think about death, but it is actually unhealthy to live in denial of death and not consider what is inevitable. Only an unwise person would go through life unprepared for what we all know will eventually happen. The writer of Hebrews states, "It is appointed unto men once to die . . ." (9:27), the question then becomes, what next? What happens after we die? Do we just turn to dust and ashes as many believe? Are we reincarnated as some preach? Or does Heaven and hell really exist, as the Bible teaches us. Jesus taught against reincarnation and spoke of a life that is condemned to eternal damnation in hell. He said:

There was a certain rich man, which was clothed in purple and fine linen, and fared sumptuously every day: And there was a certain beggar named Lazarus, which was laid at his gate, full of sores, and desiring to be fed with the crumbs which fell from the rich man's table: moreover the dogs came and licked his sores. And it came to pass, that **the beggar died, and was carried by the angels into** Abraham's bosom: the rich man also died, and was buried; And in hell he lift up his eyes being in torment, and seeth Abraham afar off, and Lazarus in his bosom. (Luke 16:19-23).

When Jesus told this parable,[1] he was talking to the Pharisees.[2]The Bible says, "And the Pharisees also, who were covetous, heard all these things: and they derided him" (Luke 16:14; KJV). The Life Application Bible puts it this way: "The Pharisees, who loved money, heard all this and were sneering at Jesus" (Luke 16:14). The Bible tells us the Pharisees loved money. In the previous verses, Jesus had just said to them, "You cannot serve both God and money" (Luke 16:13). Then Jesus tells the Pharisees the parable of Lazarus and the rich man.

He begins the parable with, "a certain rich man." He proceeds to mention the apparel of the rich man and the man's living conditions, as well. The Pharisees would have known the rich man was wealthy because purple clothing was very expensive in Biblical times. Also, the Pharisees probably knew Jesus was referring to them in this parable. They knew Jesus always spoke in parables to make a spiritual and a practical point.

Then Jesus tells of a poor man named Lazarus. This man Lazarus was so poor that he had to beg for food to eat. Lazarus probably was unable to work because of an illness, which left him full of sores. To point out how sick Lazarus was, Jesus said dogs came by and licked the sores on his body. Therefore, he must have been too weak to prevent this detestable act. This would have left him susceptible to diseases, and the Pharisees probably would have believed Lazarus was too unclean to be in the rich man's presence. Jesus tells of Lazarus' desire. It seems obvious Lazarus needs a doctor and healing. But, Jesus does not say the beggar's desire was to see a doctor or to get healed; the sick man's desire was to eat. He was so hungry he just wanted to eat the crumbs that fell from the rich man's table. Lazarus could have been close to starving to death, and apparently, the pains of hunger were more desirous than seeing a doctor for the infectious and unclean sores eating away at his body.

As Jesus continues, he stated that the the two men died. When Lazarus died, he was carried away by angels into Abraham's bosom (Luke 16:22).

---

[1] "A parable compares something familiar to something unfamiliar. It helps us understand spiritual truth by using everyday objects and relationships." From the Life Application Bible New International Version. p.1676

[2] Pharisees were a Jewish religious group that followed the Old Testament laws and their own religious traditions. They were highly respected but they hated Jesus because he challenged their attitudes and motives. Life Application Bible. p.1732.

Jesus mentions no burial for Lazarus. But he does mention Angelic escorts who were believed to accompany a soul to Abraham's bosom, the place where the righteous were kept after death according to Jewish beliefs. The rich man also died. Unlike Lazarus, Jesus does not mention angels escorting him. But Jesus does mention the rich man's burial which he could probably afford because of his status and wealth. But when he opens his eyes, he is in hell and is being tormented.

And he cried and said, Father Abraham, have mercy on me, and send Lazarus, that he may dip the tip of his finger in water, and cool my tongue; for I am tormented in this flame. But Abraham said, Son, remember that thou in thy lifetime receivedst thy good things, and likewise Lazarus evil things; but now he is comforted, and thou art tormented. And beside all this, between us and you there is a great gulf fixed: so that they which would pass from hence to you cannot; neither can they pass to us, that would come from thence (Luke 16:24-26).

In this parable, Jesus is letting us know that we will be cognizant after death. The rich man is aware of what has happened to him. He is in torment and has the capabilities of his senses. The rich man is able to see and hear Lazarus. While in torment, he seeks mercy from the man to whom he showed no mercy or compassion. Abraham reminds the rich man of his lack of compassion during his lifetime toward Lazarus. Then Abraham tells the rich man the space between them will not allow Lazarus to assist him.

This passage is one of many in the Bible that tells us about hell. In fact, the Bible has more than fifty references on hell: The apostle Matthew wrote, "And fear not them which kill the body, but are not able to kill the soul: but rather fear him which is able to destroy both soul and body in **hell**" (Matthew 10:28). John stated, "And death and **hell** were cast into the Lake of Fire" (Revelation 20:14). John further writes, "I am he that liveth, and was dead; and, behold, I am alive for evermore, Amen; and have the keys of **hell** and of death" (Revelation 1:18).

In contrast, however, there are over six hundred references in the Bible on heaven. In Psalms we read that, "The LORD is in his holy temple, the LORD's throne is in **heaven** . . ." (Psalm 11:14). The writer also asserts that "The LORD looked down from **heaven** upon the children of men, to see if there were any that did understand, and seek God" (Psalm 14:2). Finally, John the Baptist bare record, saying, I saw the Spirit descending from **heaven** like a dove, and it abode upon him" (John 1:32).

Yes, my friend, whether you believe it or not, there is a heaven and there is a hell. And depending on the decision you make today will determine where you will spend eternity. You will spend eternity in one place or the other. You must make a decision! The most important decision you could ever make is the decision to turn your back on your sinful nature and begin to follow God by accepting His Son Jesus. God desires for you to repent and turn from your wicked ways (Acts 8:22). Repentance is so very important because it gives you a clearer view of what God expects for your life.

In the following pages, we will examine the definition and biblical view on the principle of repentance. We will also explore scriptural, as well as contemporary, experiences of repentance, and finally, we will look at actions and prayers of repentance to discover what God expects and the rewards for a repentant heart.

Chapter One

A CHANGED HEART

". . . Repent ye: for the kingdom of heaven is at hand."
(Matthew 3:2)

Every believer should be baptized before beginning their ministry to reconcile others to the Father. Both Matthew and Mark records Jesus preaching repentance after His baptism in the Jordan River (Matthew 3:14-17; Mark 1:9-11). What is baptism? Baptism is a church ordinance, it is an outward rite Christ has appointed to be observed by the church (Mark 16:15-18; Matthew 28:18-20). In other words, it is an outward expression to an inward confession of a changed heart to Christ. After confessing to Christ a need for salvation from sins and asking him to live in the heart, the believer should be baptized. Baptism is an essential part of the Christian experience. The word baptism comes from the Greek verb baptize meaning, to dip, immerse, or submerge. This rite is done by believers in the Body of Christ to express their decision of a committed life to Christ. It is an ordinance commanded in the New Testament but is not required for salvation.

There are three baptisms mentioned in the Bible: the baptism into Christ and into His body, which is the church (Romans 6:4; 12:4-5; 1 Corinthians 10:17); water baptism (Matthew 28:19; Acts 2:38; 8:35-38);

and baptism into the Holy Spirit (Joel 2:28-29; John 14:12-17; Acts 1:4-8). We are first baptized into the body of Christ. Once we accept Jesus as our Savior, we should be baptized in water. After we have been baptized in water, we should then ask for God's baptism of His Holy Spirit, There have been some, however, who have received the baptism of the Holy Spirit before being water baptized.

As mentioned in my previous book, *10 Things God Expects*, "The Holy Spirit is the third person of the Godhead. He is addressed in the Bible as the Holy Ghost or the Holy Spirit over ninety times throughout the Bible. God desires for His people to have his precious gift, the Holy Spirit. When His people receive the gift of the Holy Spirit, they are able to do great exploits. Jesus told the disciples to wait for the promise of the Father, saying: "For John truly baptized with water; but ye shall be baptized with the Holy Ghost . . ." (Acts 1:5). Later he told them, "ye shall receive power, after that the Holy Ghost is come upon you: and ye shall be witnesses unto me both in Jerusalem, and in all Judaea, and in Samaria, and unto the uttermost part of the earth" (Acts 1:8). After repentance and water baptism, God gives the Holy Spirit to those of us who ask of Him. Peter in the book of Acts said: "Repent, and be baptized every one of you in the name of Jesus Christ for the remission of sins, and ye shall receive the gift of the Holy Ghost. For the promise is unto you and to your children, and to all that are afar off, even as many as the Lord our God shall call" (Acts 2:38-39). After receiving the gift of the Holy Ghost, our Lord will lead us and guide us in the way we should go. He will also reprove us on those daily things we need to repent from. As we are growing in Christ, we will find that repentance is not a onetime act.

Many believe salvation is the first principle Christ teaches at the beginning of his ministry. But it is not. The first teachings that the Son of God spoke on is the act of repentance. Repentance is much more than just acknowledging what we have done wrong. It is a change of mind and heart. It is a turning away from our sinful nature. It is also a turning away from sinful acts of wrong doing we commit against ourselves, against others and against God. Repentance also requires turning to God asking forgiveness and surrendering to His way.

Repent is used three different ways in the New Testament. The Greek words which are used: *metanoeo:* means a change for the better, an amendment, or 'repentance' from sin; *Metamelomai:* signifies 'to regret or to repent oneself; and *metanoia:* means as an afterthought, change of mind from sin or evil. However, in the Old Testament, all these expressions are encapsulated by one verb the Hebrew word *shuv* meaning "to turn and return." This root combines both fundamentals of repentance: to turn from evil and to turn to good. The motion of turning implies a change in direction from the current path. God has given all men the power to redirect his or her destiny. The story of the Prodigal Son, is a great example of a disobedient and sinful son who repents or turns from evil and redirects his destiny.

In Luke 15:11-32 we read that there was a certain man who had two sons and Jesus explains: "The younger of them said to his father, Father, give me the portion of goods that falleth to me. And he divided unto them his living. And not many days after the younger son gathered all together, and took his journey into a far country, and there wasted his substance with riotous living" (Luke 15:12-13).

How many of God's children today are just like the Prodigal Son? How many of God's children walked away from the church and have journeyed into Satan's kingdom? And how many of God's children are selfishly wasting their God-giving time, talent, substance and life on "riotous" living? They are recklessly spending and wasting the resources God provides for them by using them on things that will not benefit the kingdom of God. Whenever we use what God has given us on ungodliness, it is sin (Titus 3:1-11). If this is the path you have taken, dear reader, then it is time to repent. We all sin and we are all born in sin and shaped in iniquity therefore all of us sin. The scriptures affirm this in the following manner, "For all have sinned, and come short of the glory of God" (Psalm 65:3; Romans 3:23). It is our sin nature that causes us to live contrary to the will of God (Ephesians 2:1-10).

God understood we had no power over sin that is why he sent His Son, Jesus, to die for our sins. The Bible states: For God so loved the world that he gave his only begotten Son, that whosoever believeth in him should not perish, but have everlasting life. For God sent not his Son into the world to condemn the world; but that the world through him might be saved; so that their eyes would be opened and that they would turn from darkness to light, and from the power of Satan unto God, that they may receive forgiveness of sins, and inheritance among them which are sanctified by faith that is in Jesus (John 3:15-17, Acts 26:18). God is merciful He hath not dealt with us after our sins; nor rewarded us according to our iniquities (Psalm 103:10). He is waiting for you to repent.

The Prodigal son spent all that his father gave him on foolishness and found himself in a place of humiliation and shame. And when he had spent all, there arose a mighty famine in that land; and he began to be in want. And he went and joined himself to a citizen of that country; and he sent him into his fields to feed swine. And he would fain (happy, willing) have filled his belly with the husks that the swine did eat: and no man gave unto him (Luke 15:14-16).

This son had clearly forgotten who He was and where He had come from. A Jew happily feeding and thinking about eating swine was forbidden under the Levitical Law. Moses wrote, "Of their flesh shall ye not eat, and their carcass shall ye not touch; they are unclean to you." (Leviticus 11:8) Yet, like this young man many of God's children are out of place. They are living in sin and willingly working in the Devil's vineyard and happily eating his delicacies, while the Devil is killing, stealing, and destroying God's plan for their lives (John 10:10). The Bible clearly states: "For the wages of sin is death . . ." (Romans 6:23a).

And when he came to himself, he said, How many hired servants of my father's have bread enough and to spare, and I perish with hunger! I will arise and go to my father, and will say unto him, Father; I have sinned against heaven, and before thee, and am no more worthy to be called thy son: make me as one of thy hired servants (Luke 15:17-19).The son is in the first stage of repentance, in other words, he is in the thinking stage. He now has a moment of sanity, and begins thinking back to the days when he was in his father's house. Jesus does not say how long he thought about going back. But Jesus does say that the man thought about the servants in his father's house. He thought about his current position and recognized how much better off his father's servants were than he. He thought about what he would say to his father. He thought about how unworthy he felt and how undeserving he was to be elevated as his son. He became willing and humbled to become a hired servant. As a servant, he understood he would follow, listen to, and obey instructions. When we humble ourselves to Jesus and repent, we become His servants (John 15:15). Jesus expects us to follow Him by reading, listening to, and obeying His Word (Matthew 16:24; Mark 4:9; Luke 4:4). What a blessing to know that when we humble ourselves to our Lord, and truly repent and turn toward Him, our Savior is always there to accept us as His own. The Lord is always waiting with His arms open wide "God commendeth his love toward us, in that, while we were yet sinners, Christ died for us" (Romans 5:8). Christ died for us so we would have access to the throne of Grace (Hebrews 4:16).

The Prodigal son, after thinking about his situation ". . . arose, and went to his father's house" (Luke 15:20). This is the action stage of repentance. Repentance requires action. He got up, turned from the pig's pen and began to return to his father's house. This is a clear indication of repentance, walking away from the old life and turning toward his new life in Christ. Your actions always follows your thoughts. Whenever one turns away from sin and calls on Jesus, He will hear them. He said, "Call unto me, and I will answer thee, and shew thee great and mighty things, which thou knowest not." (Jeremiah 33:3). God said when you turn away from your sin and turn to Him, "Then shalt thou call, and the Lord shall answer; thou shalt cry and he shall say here I am . . ." (Isaiah 58:9a). The Father promised his children "For whosoever shall call upon the name of the Lord shall be saved" (Romans 10:13).

When the Prodigal son was yet a great way off, his father saw him, and had compassion, and ran, and fell on his neck, and kissed him. And the son said unto him, Father, I have sinned against heaven, and in thy sight, and am no more worthy to be called thy son (Luke 15:20-21).

Confession of sin and accepting Christ as Lord, is the third and final step of repentance. This is an important part of repentance because you are telling God you recognize that you are unclean and in need of a Savior. The Bible states, if you confess your sins, He is faithful and just to forgive you of your sins and cleanse you of all unrighteousness (John 1:9). The Father sent the Son to be the Savior of the world. Whosoever shall confess that Jesus is the Son of God, God dwelleth in him, and he in God (1 John 4:14-15). It is important to note that "If thou confess with thy mouth the Lord Jesus, and shalt believe in thine heart that God hath raised him from the dead, thou shalt be saved. For with the heart man believeth unto righteousness; and with the mouth confession is made unto salvation" (Romans 10:9-10).

The Prodigal Son repented. He had a change of mind and a change of heart. He thought about who he was, where he was, and where he could be. This knowledge caused him to call on his father and then he decided it was time to change his position. He then confessed his sins and faults and came to understand that his father was always there for him waiting for his return. Our heavenly Father is as loving and patient as well and He awaits the repentance and return of His sons and daughters.

But the father said to his servants, Bring forth the best robe, and put it on him; and put a ring on his hand, and shoes on his feet: And bring hither the fatted calf, and kill it; and let us eat, and be merry: For this my son was dead, and is alive again; he was lost, and is found. And they began to be merry.

It has been said that the angels in heaven rejoice when a child of God repents and turns his back on sin. God loves His children so much, and he is always ready to pardon them for their sins. God is gracious and merciful, slow to anger and of great kindness. (Nehemiah 9:17b). He is waiting and calling you today, dear reader, to return to Him and repent.

Chapter Two

THE TEMPTED HEART

Against thee, only, have I sinned,
and done this evil in thy sight:
(Psalms 51:4)

In chapter one, we established what it means to have a change of heart and repent. We now understand anyone walking contrary to the Word of God can and should repent. They should turn back to their heavenly Father who sent his only begotten Son to die on the cross for the sins of the world. The Bible tells us the Father sent His Son, Jesus, not to condemn the world; but that the world through Him might be saved (John 3:16-17). Jesus said, if we believe and accept his Spirit and His Words, then the Father will accept us. Also in chapter one, we read on the stages of repentance. We understand that whenever we make a decision to change, turn back to, and confess our sins to the Father, the Father forgives us. With loving kindness and tender mercies, He is always waiting for his wayward children to repent, and with arms stretched out wide He will embrace and forgive each one who does. Make the choice today to turn from sin and return to the One who loves you and is able to give you a new life. Just as the Prodigal Son returned to his father whose arms were opened wide, our heavenly Father is always there for us with His arms opened wide when we turn and repent.

In this chapter we will discuss temptation, where it comes from, where it could lead us and how to overcome its power. It is the desire of God that His children repent and live in union with Him. God loves us so much that He sent Jesus to show us how to live victoriously and abundantly (1 Corinthians 15:7; John 10:10). Before Jesus came into the world in human flesh, the enemies of God, Satan and all of his followers, had God's people in bondage. Who is Satan? Satan, also known as Lucifer, is a fallen angel (Isaiah 14:12). This angelic being was in heaven with God; but because of pride he thought he could exalt himself to be like God (Isaiah 14:13-16). The Bible tells us that Satan is the accuser of the brethren, (Job 1:6-11); he tries to block our blessings, (Zechariah 3:1-10); he tries to tempt us and to get us to tempt God, (Matthew 4:3-11); he will try to steal the Word from our heart by fear, doubt, unbelief, and deceit (Mark 4:13-19; Acts 5:2-4); he tries to hinder us from doing the work of God, (1 Thessalonians 2:18); he tries to hinder our prayers, (1 Peter 3:7). Satan can also try to oppress a person or possess them (Luke 13:16; 23:3). The word of God tells us not to give "place to the devil" (Ephesians. 4:27); but, to put on God's armor so we will be able "to stand against the wiles of the devil" (Ephesians 6:10-18). We should not be ignorant of "his devices" (2 Corinthians 2:11), and always submit to God, "resist the devil," and the devil will flee (James 4:7; 1 Peter 5:8). These facts prove we can expect opposition from Satan and his army but we have God on our side if we have accepted his Son. Therefore, when we are tempted in our hearts, we can trust and believe God's word.

The Lord knew that in our sinful flesh we were no match for Satan's tricks and deceptions. Jesus was sent to save us from the chains that held us in bondage, the temptations that kept us in sin, and the thoughts that kept us blinded from the truth. Nevertheless, after the beating and bruising of his body, his death, burial, resurrection, and ascension, Jesus, who went to sit at the right hand of the Father, sent back the Holy Spirit. We now have God's Spirit living and dwelling in our mortal bodies giving us power and authority over all the traps and influences of the enemy.

Temptation from the enemy is no match for us without the Holy Spirit. One of the greatest kings in the Bible, of whom the Lord said is "a man after mine own heart," was overcome by and unable to withstand great temptations (Acts 13:22). But God knew King David had a repentant heart. Whenever David realized he had fallen into the snare of the enemy, he would seek God's face. David trusted God. He knew God would not forsake him. He wrote, "They that know thy name will put their trust in thee: for thou, LORD, hast not forsaken them that seek thee" (Psalm 9:10). David's prayer of repentance in Psalm 51 shows a man who is willing to turn his back on sin and give his whole heart to his God. David was broken and bewildered because of the sin he had committed. He had lust in his heart after another man's wife, and ultimately committed adultery with her. When she became pregnant by King David, he tried to deceive and trick the husband to sleep with his wife. When the man refused because of his devotion to his king and his country, he returned to the battlefield; at which point, King David had the man murdered (2 Samuel 11). God then sent the prophet, Nathan to the king to remind David that God saved him from Saul, gave him the house of Israel and Judah, and would have given him much more if he had asked; so why would he sin in the sight of God? Just as God reminded the king of his provisions, kindness and love, the Lord reminds His children today of the same. The Lord is asking His children today, 'Why, with all that I have done for you and all that I have given to you, would you sin in my sight? I would have given you anything you asked for, yet you choose to follow after the way of the world. Turn today and repent. Turn away from your life of sin and return unto me, and I will have mercy on you and forgive you of your sins. Give me your heart and I will take care of you because I love you. "Repent!" The voice of the Lord has spoken. David heard the voice of the Lord and he repented saying:

> Have mercy upon me, O God, according to thy loving kindness: according unto the multitude of thy tender mercies blot out my transgressions. Wash me throughly from mine iniquity, and cleanse me from my sin. For I acknowledge my transgressions: and my sin is ever before me. (Psalm 51:1-3).

David first asks for mercy and understands that God is a merciful God. David also recognizes himself as sinful and unable to save himself. As you reflect on your behaviors, attitudes, and actions today do you recognize your sinful nature? Do you realize that when you walk contrary to the word of God you are transgressing against God? Do you understand that God is a merciful God and is slow to anger? David did, so he then asks a request from God to wash him and cleanse him. David realizes his transgressions against God and so he says,

"Against thee, thee only, have I sinned, and done this evil in thy sight: that thou mightest be justified when thou speakest, and be clear when thou judgest" (Psalm 51:4).

David speaks the truth to his heavenly Father. He realizes that God has given him so much, compassion, mercy, and wealth and he turned his back on God. He knew the commandments; he knew God's ways and his works. So David had believed God would be justified in judging him. As you read this, are you reflecting on the many blessings God has given you? Have you walked contrary to the commandments of God? Would God be justified in judging you? David pleaded his cause by saying, "Behold, I was shaped in iniquity; and in sin did my mother conceive me." (Psalm 51:5). David says look, I am a sinful, evil, wicked creature and have been since birth. These tendencies have overtaken me and have ruled my life, these things are in me. Ask yourself the question, what things are in you that demonstrate you are sinful, evil and wicked? Do you see yourself as such a person? How would a holy and righteous God see you? David said:

> Behold, thou desirest truth in the inward parts: and in the hidden part thou shalt make me to know wisdom. Purge me with hyssop, and I shall be clean: wash me, and I shall be whiter than snow (Psalm 51:6-7).

David acknowledges that he understands what God wants but it is not in him to give it. But he lets God know that He is the Mighty One, the One who is able to purge, wash, and make him clean and is able to give him the wisdom and strength to do what is right. Do you realize you are unable to break some of the demonic addictions or behaviors you have without the help of the Lord. You must be willing to admit and submit to the all Powerful One. The One who is able to purge you, wash you, and make you clean. Jesus is able to give you the strength you need to be free from the bondage you are under.

David asked God to purge him with hyssop. Hyssop is a plant the Jews used for purification rites. The leaves were used to paint blood over their doors to remember the Passover. (Read Exodus 7-12). David wanted the Lord to wash him, purify him, and cleanse him from his sins. Our heavenly Father sent his Son into the world to shed his blood so that we would be washed, purified, justified, and cleansed by the blood of Jesus (I Corinthians 6:11; Revelation 12:11).

> Make me to hear joy and gladness; that the bones which thou hast broken may rejoice. Hide thy face from my sins, and blot out all mine iniquities. Create in me a clean heart, O God; and renew a right spirit within me (Psalm 51:8-10).

David sounds very sorrowful and desirous for the Lord to restore his joy and gladness because of the guilt he was probably enduring. David was also asking the Lord to overlook his sinful self and take away his sinful nature. Then he asks the Father to give him a fresh and new start with a right spirit and clean heart. David is asking for a new heart, a clean one. He understands God is the only one, the Creator of the universe, who can cleanse the heart. You can almost hear David's cry and feel his heaviness asking for a fresh start. Have you cried out to the Lord or are you comfortable walking in sin and walking contrary to the word of God. David continues:

> Cast me not away from thy presence; and take not thy holy spirit from me. Restore unto me the joy of thy salvation; and uphold me with thy free spirit. Then will I teach transgressors thy ways; and sinners shall be converted unto thee. (Psalm 51:11-13).

The king has lost his zeal for life. He has lost his joy. He does not want to be cast out from the presence of God. He asks the Lord not to take His Holy Spirit from him. David pleads for the joy he once knew in salvation. David says only then will I be able to teach others your ways and see them convert back to you. Can you teach the commandments of God with a clean heart and clear conscious? Are you able to tell others how to live in the sight of God without being convicted? Do you still have the joy and the excitement you once had while sharing the Gospel? If not, perhaps you should ask God to restore the joy of your salvation.

> Deliver me from blood guiltiness, O God, thou God of my salvation: and my tongue shall sing aloud of thy righteousness. O Lord, open thou my lips; and my mouth shall shew forth thy praise. For thou desirest not sacrifice; else would I give it: thou delightest not in burnt offering. The sacrifices of God are a broken spirit: a broken and a contrite heart, O God, thou wilt not despise. (Psalm 51:14-17).

David asks God for deliverance to be able to sing aloud of God's righteousness and to be able to praise God once more. David is willing to praise God aloud and give sacrifices and burnt offerings to show forth his works before God. However, he understands that God is not looking for the works we do but rather looking at the heart and the spirit of a man. God takes pleasure in a heart that is humbled before him. This is the sacrifice God is looking for in a heart that repents.

Chapter Three

THE DECEITFUL HEART

"The heart is deceitful above all things and desperately wicked . . ."
(Jeremiah 17:9)

While in graduate school, one professor asked each student to research two domestic or international issues. Classes were held online and my classmates lived in five of the seven continents. It was a unique program and very informative because the class discussions were on grassroots issues around the world. One of the stories I will never forget was introduced by a classmate from South Africa. He shared with the class babies under the age of five raped in South Africa is a thing of concern for many. Every day, he said, the newspapers bring awful revelations of the number of men due to appear in court, accused of raping little girls. He said, one five year-old girl was discovered covered in blood and in tears. He mentioned in class, it is the latest in a series of rapes of baby girls—some of them involving children less than one year-old, which has left South Africans reeling with horror. A number of high profile baby rapes since 2001 he stated, increased the need to address the problem socially and legally. He also mentioned, a 9-month-old baby was raped by six men, between the ages of 24 and 66 and a 4-year-old girl died after being raped by her father. He also said, a 14-month-old girl was raped by her two uncles. Then he mentioned, in February 2002, an 8-month-old infant was reportedly gang raped by four men and only one has been charged. He stated sadly, the infant required extensive reconstructive surgery to rebuild urinary, genital, abdominal, and tracheal systems. The 8-month-old infant's injuries, he said, were so extensive increased attention on prosecution has occurred.

This story shocked me and shook me to the core of my being. The raping of infants and children (in this region), may be attributed to the belief by the local people that sex with a child or baby will cure HIV/AIDS. I was horrified. I continued to wonder why and how men can be void of any moral and spiritual substance, and be so deceived, that they can believe, if they have intercourse with an infant they would be healed of HIV/AIDS. I cried. My heart was so heavy I prayed for peace. I also prayed that the light of the gospel would shine in that region where little infant girls are being brutalized and destroyed physically, emotionally, and even killed before they can speak. Why, in this day, can this kind of belief and behavior be displayed in the minds of men? How is it that the hearts of men can be so evil? How is it that men could do such horrific things and never bat an eye nor think about whether he is in error? These questions continued to haunt me as I looked for answers in the Word of God to find out why men and women can be so deceived.

The Bible states that their minds are blinded. Why, because the "god of this world hath **blinded** [their] **minds** . . . lest the light of the glorious gospel of Christ, who is the image of God, should shine unto them (2 Corinthians 4:4). In Timothy we read that in the latter times, some will be giving heed to **seducing spirits** . . . and their **conscience seared** with a hot iron and hearts harden to the truth! (2 Corinthians 3:14; 1 Tim 4:1b-2). Jeremiah, one of the Old Testament prophets said, "The **heart is deceitful** above all things, and desperately wicked . . ." (Jeremiah 17:9). We can all look at the situation above and believe that these men should be condemned because of their abominable act toward these babies; however, God sees all sin as offensive, 1 John 5:17 states that all unrighteousness is sin. In the book of Isaiah we read, "All our righteousness is as filthy rags" (Isaiah 64:6). In the New Testament, the Apostle Paul writes that all of us sin, stating: "For all have sinned and come short of the glory of God" (Romans 3:23). If you say you do not sin, you are deceived (1 John 1:8).

We as humans tend to see sin on a scale of what is acceptable and what is unacceptable. God does not place a numerical scale on sin, nor does he rate it. There is no little sin or big sin, it is all sin in God's eyes. The man that has robbed the bank is no more justified in God's sight than the man who steals a candy bar from the store. The man who kills in a bar-room brawl is no more justified in the sight of God than the man who goes on a serial killing spree. The man who lies to the government on his taxes is no more justified than the man who lies to his wife regarding his adulterous affair. These are all sinful acts according to God's commandments and the Bible says the "wages of sin is death . . ." (Romans 6:23). Sin is sin. Many have been deceived in believing wrong is right if it does not hurt anyone. But that is what is called deception; and the root cause of deception is disobedience to divine authority. There is no real submission to God's Word or His Spirit.

Additionally, there are some that believe they are good people and God sees them as righteous and good. Some believe because of their good works God favors them. No he does not! Remember, God said in His Word that: "We are all as an unclean thing, and all of our righteousness is as filthy rags" in His sight (Isaiah 64:6). "There is none righteous, no, not one" (Romans 3:10).

One of Satan's tricks is to deceive God's people to believe if we are good enough we can get into heaven. According to the Bible, just being good is not the way to get into heaven. If you interviewed a thousand people from around the world and ask each one of them, if they have ever lied, stole anything, looked at another person with lust in their heart or condemned anyone with their tongue, more than likely all of them would say yes to all four. If you would ask them if they believe in God and the devil or heaven and hell, a large majority of them would probably say yes. If you then ask them if they believe they are going to heaven or hell, many will probably say heaven. They may say they do not believe they are going to hell because overall, they are good people. Many people think just because they are good, they will make it into heaven but the Bible is contrary to this thought. The bible says that all our righteousness is like filthy rags in the sight of God and the unrighteous will not see the Kingdom of God. God is righteous and He desires that His creation live victoriously on earth and live in eternity with Him that is why he made provisions through His Son, Christ Jesus.

It is the desire of God that all men are saved and that none be lost but all would come into the knowledge of the truth (I Timothy 2:3-:4). For the Scriptures states there is one God, and one mediator between God and men, the man Christ Jesus (1Timothy 2:3-5). God loves His people so much and He wants to have a relationship with all men as He did with

Adam. So in order to do that, He needed a sacrificial lamb to die for their sins. The Old Testament priest would take a lamb and sprinkle the blood on the bronze altar for the sins of the Israelites; and once a year, the High Priest whom God had set apart for Himself would enter the Holy of Holies to sprinkle blood on the mercy seat for the sins of the nation of Israel (Hebrews 7:26-27). But God in His mercy and grace sent Jesus to not only abolish the law but also to die on the cross for all men's sins (1 Corinthians 15:3-4). He did this so His creation would trust and serve Him and not perish. The Bible says, "For God so loved the world, that he gave his only begotten Son, that whosoever believeth in him should not perish, but have everlasting life. For God sent not his Son into the world to condemn the world; but that the world through him might be saved" (John 3:16-17). Saved from what? We are saved from eternal damnation and can have everlasting life (John 3:15). We are saved from the curse of the law and therefore can be free from sin, sickness, disease, and poverty and live an abundant life (John 10:10).

Finally, we are saved from the bondage of darkness and can now walk in God's marvelous light (Matthew 6:23; Luke 1:79). No longer do we have to be deceived by the power of darkness. No longer do we have to be deceived by the tricks of the enemy. No longer do we have to be deceived by the snares of the devil. No longer do we have to disobey divine authority. We have been set free from the lust of the flesh, lust of the eye, and the pride of life (1 John 2:15-17). No longer are we enslaved to sin, but now we have been set free from sin and can become servants to God by His grace (Romans 6:14). He gave us a gift and that gift is abundant life through Jesus Christ our Lord (John 10:10). Once you escape sin and you no longer have to listen to sin tell you what to do, and you are able to hear God's voice and follow His lead, what a delightful blessing. Men all over the world no longer have to be deceived by the enemy's lies. Men no longer have to be ensnared by the tricks of the devil. No longer do they have to be destroyed by Satan's scare tactics. Abundant and eternal life is for all those who repent when they turn from their life of sin, and then return to their heavenly Father. No matter what you have done and how deep you believe you are in a situation that you cannot get out of, your loving Father is waiting for you to repent. Come dear sinner, come and repent.

Chapter Four

THE DOUBTFUL HEART

And immediately Jesus stretched forth his hand,
and caught him, and said unto him,
O thou of little faith, wherefore didst thou doubt?
Matt 14:31

We must understand that repentance is a blessing because it offers sinners a new start. Jesus, himself, presents it as a priority, not an option; the choice given to sinners is either "repent or perish (Luke 13:3). God ". . . is not willing that any should perish, but that all should come to repentance" (2 Peter 3:9). Jesus, while speaking to the scribes and Pharisees told them His mission saying, "I came not to call the righteous, but sinners to repentance." (Mark 2:17). He said, "Repent, for the kingdom of heaven is at hand" (Matthew 4:17). Moreover, right before Jesus' ascension, He told His disciples to preach repentance to all people saying, "Repentance and remission of sins should be preached in His name among all nations . . ." (Luke 24:47). Even though believers share the message of repentance to sinners, there is no guarantee that one would turn from their sinful ways and begin to trust the Lord. The Scribes, Pharisees, Sadducees and the lawyers of Jesus' time prove this very point. These men always doubted who He was; they were always questioning His authority and tempting Him to prove Himself. In Matthew 9:ll, they questioned Jesus about who he ate with; In Mark 8:11, they tempted Jesus to give them a sign from heaven; In Luke 5:33 and 6:2, they questioned Him about fasting and praying and breaking the law on the Sabbath; and in John 8:3-6, they attempted to accuse Jesus of error in the Scriptures. Jesus knew their thoughts and the evil in their hearts (Matthew 9:4). In Matthew 23:13-36 and Luke 11:39-54, Jesus calls them hypocrites, blind guides, and fools and told them they were full of hypocrisy and iniquity. Not only did the leaders during Jesus' time doubt him, but some of his family and friends did as well. The Bible records: ". . . For neither did his brethren believe in him" (John 7:3-5). And in John 10:24 we read, "The Jews said to Him, 'How long dost thou make us to doubt? If thou be the Christ, tell us plainly'" (John 10:24).

Doubting God and lacking confidence in His word and His works is a trait that has been exemplified in the lives of God's people throughout the Bible. Why? Why is it that the people of God doubt Him? What is in the heart of man that he will question God's word and His works? We know that Satan blinds the minds of men to doubt in their hearts and hinder them from coming into the full knowledge of God (2 Corinthians 4:4). The fear of the unknown oftentimes leaves the sinner in a state of uncertainty, as well. Additionally, the fear of letting go of deeply held ideas is another reason why a person would doubt the message of God. Doubting that Jesus is the way, or doubting that he can bring about a change in one's life after repentance, can leave a person feeling very unsure about turning from their old ways. It is not uncommon for sinners or the people of God to doubt His existence, doubt that they are loved by Him, or doubt that they even need Him. Jesus said, do not be of a doubtful mind" (Luke 12:29). He said, ". . . the kingdom of God is at hand: repent ye, and believe the gospel" (Mark 1:15). He said, I am the way, the truth and the life, no man comes to the Father except by me. This chapter will look at two men who knew Jesus personally yet they had doubts and expressed them. We will also answer the question: why should the doubtful heart be changed?

There are many stories in the Bible that speak of how and why God's people doubted Him. The one person that would come to the minds of many when we bring up the word doubt is Thomas. Thomas was one of Jesus' disciples that doubted much of everything that anyone said or did. He was nicknamed doubting Thomas for this reason. Let us look at Thomas' life.

The first time we see Thomas is in the book of Matthew 10:3. He is sixth in the lineup of the twelve disciples. We then hear him voicing his opinion in the book of John, chapter 11. This chapter opens with Mary and Martha sending for Jesus because their brother Lazarus was very sick. When Jesus heard Lazarus was sick, he did not leave to see about him right away. But two days later when Jesus decides to go to Lazarus, his disciples remind him that the Jews there want to kill Him. When Jesus explains it is not His time to die, Lazarus is dead, and he must go to raise him up, Thomas said, "unto his fellow disciples, Let us also go, that we may die with him" (ll:16). Now Jesus had already said what would happen, but Thomas doubts the Master's words. How many times have you heard the Word of God, dear reader, and doubted it or did not heed to the call to repent? How many times have you felt the tug on your heart and refused to open your heart fully to the Lord? Jesus understands our fears and doubts. Yet, He still calls saying, come my child, repent.

The next time we read about Thomas is in the book of John. Many of the disciples had seen Jesus after His resurrection but Thomas was not with them. When they told Thomas, they had seen Jesus he was very doubtful. John records it this way:

But Thomas, one of the twelve, called Didymus, was not with them when Jesus came. The other disciples therefore said unto him, we have seen the LORD. But he said unto them, except I shall see in his hands the print of the nails, and put my finger into the print of the nails, and thrust my hand into his side, I will not believe.

Thomas was a disciple of Jesus who had been there when Jesus healed the sick. He was also there when Jesus, "gave [the disciples] power against unclean spirits, to cast them out, and to heal all manner of sickness and all manner of disease" (Matthew 10:1). He was there when Jesus raised Lazarus from the dead (John 11:41-44). And he was there at the Last Supper, when Jesus told his disciples what was to come. Yet, after all he had heard and seen, there was still doubt in Thomas' heart (Matthew 26:26-35). Is this you dear reader? After seeing miracles take place in your own life and hearing the great things God has done in the lives of others, do you still doubt Him? But Jesus is patient; He loves His children and wants their best in life. The Bible states that He waits standing at the door of our heart knocking, saying, ". . . if any man hears my voice, and open the door, I will come in to him, and will sup with him, and he with me" (Revelation 3:20). Jesus came back to show Thomas his nail scared hands so that all his doubts would be dispelled. Thomas then repents and believes saying, "My LORD and my God" (John 20:28).

And after eight days again his disciples were within, and Thomas with them: then came Jesus, the doors being shut, and stood in the midst, and said, Peace be unto you. Then saith he to Thomas, Reach hither thy finger, and behold my hands; and reach hither thy hand, and thrust it into my side: and be not faithless, but believing. And Thomas answered and said unto him, My LORD and my God . . . (John 20:24-29).

Thomas is like many of us who doubt Jesus' resurrection power before believing it. There is nothing wrong with that especially as a newborn Christian. Jesus is merciful and he wants to dismiss all your doubts. Jesus smiles and with his arms opened wide He is saying see my blood stained hands, feel the scar on my side, and behold the holes in my feet, it was all for you my child. I did it all for you and now I ask you to trust me, believe me, turn from your sinful ways and doubting thoughts, and repent. If you ask Jesus to reveal Himself to you, He will. He wants to dispel all your fears and doubts so you will believe Him, trust Him, and doubt not.

Then Jesus ends by telling Thomas "because thou hast seen me, thou hast believed: blessed are they that have not seen, and yet have believed." In other words, Jesus is saying to all those who did not literally see Him and can believe God's word; if they can believe that God loved them so much to send His only begotten Son to die for them, and if they can believe that Christ lived and was crucified for them, and if they can believe Christ died on the cross and was buried and rose from the dead, they too will be blessed. One day I heard the call to repent. I was walking down a path of unrighteousness when the Lord through His grace and mercy allowed me to see my sins and my sinful nature. A lady I met while riding on the bus in Philadelphia told me about Jesus. It was then I turned from dead works to a new life in Christ Jesus. I ask you, dear reader, do not wait any longer. Hear the voice of the Lord and repent.

Nicodemus was a man during Jesus' time that had his doubts. He had a high position of authority as a Pharisee and a member of the Sanhedrin Council, (the highest judicial council of the ancient Jewish nation). He is mentioned three times in the New Testament all recorded in the Gospel of John. His initial meeting with Jesus was at night. Nicodemus was questioning Jesus about Jesus' beliefs. Nicodemus and some of the other Pharisees discussed the works of Jesus and they believed Jesus came from God because he stated,

"Rabbi, **we** know that thou art a teacher come from God: for no man can do these miracles that thou doest, except God be with him" (John 3:2).

Then Jesus answers Nicodemus saying, "Verily, verily, I say unto thee, except a man be born again, he cannot see the kingdom of God" (John 3:3).

Nicodemus then says to Jesus, "How can a man be born when he is old? Can he enter the second time into his mother's womb, and be born (John 3:4)?"

Jesus says,

> "Verily, verily, I say unto thee, except a man be born of water and of the Spirit, he cannot enter into the kingdom of God That which is born of the flesh is flesh; and that which is born of the Spirit is spirit Marvel not that I said unto thee, Ye must be born again. The wind bloweth where it listeth, and thou hearest the sound thereof, but canst not tell whence it cometh, and whither it goeth: so is every one that is born of the Spirit" (John 3:5).

Nicodemus then ask, "How can these things be?" In other words, Nicodemus is saying, I understand that the wind blows and I can hear it. And you are right about my not knowing where the wind is going. But I doubt very seriously if a man can enter into his mother's womb a second time. How can a man be born again or how can he be born of the Spirit? It is almost like Nicodemus is saying, just speak plainly, give me the answer, and do not leave me in doubt. I want to understand. Jesus believes Nicodemus should know these things so he criticized him saying:

> Art thou a master of Israel, and knowest not these things? Verily, verily, I say unto thee, we speak that we do know, and testify that we have seen; and ye receive not our witness. If I have told you earthly things, and ye believe not, how shall ye believe, if I tell you of heavenly things? (John 3:10-12).

Jesus continues His dialogue with Nicodemus saying:

For God so loved the world, that he gave his only begotten Son, that whosoever believeth in him should not perish, but have everlasting life. For God sent not his Son into the world to condemn the world; but that the world through him might be saved. He that believeth on him is not condemned: but he that believeth not is condemned already, because he hath not believed in the name of the only begotten Son of God (John 3:16-18)

After they ended their dialogue, the next time we see Nicodemus is in a council setting. The chief priests and the Pharisees have sent officers out to arrest Jesus but they came back without him.

Then came the officers to the chief priests and Pharisees; and they said unto them, Why have ye not brought him? The officers answered, never a man spake like this man. (John 7:45-49).

The officers came back without Jesus to the chief priests and the Pharisees, and they asked why they did not have Him. The officers told them they never heard anyone speak the way Jesus spoke. The soldiers heard him speaking with power and authority (John 7:28-29). Although the Pharisees doubted Jesus, the officers did not; they appear to doubt the Pharisees reasons for wanting Jesus arrested. The Pharisees accused the officers of being deceived by Jesus. Then the chief priests said, "you do not see any rulers or Pharisees believing on this man it is the people who do not know the law that believe Him and they are cursed" (John 7:48-49). Nicodemus must have thought on the things Jesus told him because he defends Jesus or at least wanting Him to have a fair trial. Then Nicodemus speaks and says, "Doth our law judge any man, before it hear him, and know what he doeth?" (John 7:51). The priests and the Pharisees were offended and seemed cynical and agitated by what Nicodemus said because they replied, "Art thou also of Galilee? Search and look: for out of Galilee ariseth no prophet" (John 7:52). They told Nicodemus to search the Old Testament writings to prove there are no prophets coming out of Galilee. The point they were trying to make was that Jesus could not be a prophet or the Messiah as many of the people claimed because of his birth place. They believed the Messiah would come out of Bethlehem (Micah 5:2). They were unaware the birth place of Jesus was in Bethlehem (Matthew 2:1-6).

The last recording of Nicodemus, in the Bible, is in John 19:38-42. He is now burying Jesus with Joseph of Arimathaea. These men were both wealthy, both were from the Sanhedrin courts, and Joseph of Arimathaea was a disciple of Jesus. (Matthew 27:57) He begged Pilate the governor, for the body of Jesus, albeit in secret because he was afraid of the Jews (Matthew 27:58). Nevertheless, we see a bolder Nicodemus assisting Joseph of Arimathaea in the burial process while many of Jesus' disciples had fled the scene. Nicodemus brought a mixture of myrrh and aloes for the burial process and both men wrapped the body of Jesus in linen clothes, which was the custom (Matthew 27:59-60). No doubt, these two discussed their encounters with Jesus. Nicodemus probably talked about the doubts he had of Jesus. And perhaps he shared his night encounter with the Lord, as well. And undoubtedly he shared how Jesus dispelled his doubts whereby he was more willing than ever to defend Jesus against the Sanhedrin council.

Dear reader, there is an old Chinese proverb that says, "With great doubts come great understanding; with little doubts come little understanding." Jesus understand your doubts. There is much to understand in the kingdom of God and there is much to understand in the Word of God. This is your opportunity to turn your back on the sin that has you bound. This is your opportunity to dispel any doubts you have about Jesus being the Son of God. This is your opportunity to dispel all false beliefs you may have regarding the Word of God, and this is your opportunity to understand and heed to the call of the Lord to repent.

Chapter Five

AN UNBELIEVING HEART

**And he did not many mighty works there because of their unbelief
(Matthew 13:58).**

**Lord, I believe; help thou mine unbelief
(Mark 9:24).**

This chapter focuses on a heart of unbelief and how it can be changed. Have you ever talked with someone who is living in unbelief? Have you ever communicated with a person who looks at the negative side of everything? Or, have you ever met a person who just does not believe any good idea can work or any good thing can happen? I have. This kind of person does not seem to believe anything will turn out successful for them or anyone around them. It seems this type of person can complain about anything. You know that they have a difficult time believing God because they do not think anything good ever happens. Whenever they express themselves, they seem to have a negative word about everything. They have such a pessimistic attitude that, if you are around them for too long a period of time, their negativity can become infectious. It is very likely, in such surroundings, if you are not careful, you'll begin complaining with them and walk in unbelief.

I had an encounter with a young woman as an undergraduate student at Temple University. We had taken a jazz class together and after class, we would walk in the same direction to our next class. One day we were walking together and I told her some extraordinary news I had recently received. I was so excited about it; I wanted to share it with everyone I knew. I told her that a representative from Temple's Study Abroad program told me that I had been one of the ten people chosen to go to Ghana, West Africa. I knew my classmate saw everything in a negative way, but I thought she would see this news differently because, in my opinion, it was bigger than anything we had discussed.

When I told her, I was astonished that she began to speak so negatively about the trip. She started talking about the tremendous cost of the trip; she spoke negatively about the unreasonable amount of time involved. She also said there is no guarantee that the airplane would get me there safely, implying the plane may crash. She then talked about how being enclosed in an airplane for hours could make people sick. She mentioned the wars that are happening in different parts of Africa and there is the possibility of me being captured and held as a prisoner. She continued with her negative thoughts that by the time she finished talking, I sensed she had penetrated my spiritual shield. I began to feel fear and had become faint-hearted. She single-handedly, in a matter of minutes, effectively destroyed the joy I had about the trip just by using the negative force of power she had on her tongue. The negative force of her words had spiritually penetrated my heart and dissolved the joy I initially experienced.

When I realized how spiritually weak I had become, I stopped her and began to bind up every negative word she had spoken over my life. I then cast down every plot and plan of the enemy that would try to hinder the plan of God in my life. I proceeded to tell her, I will go to Africa (and I did), I will return safely (and I did), and that everything God has for me in Africa, I will receive (and I did). I began to thank God and told Him I receive his supernatural leading in my life. I also thanked Him for the supernatural blessings that he had in store for me. At this point my classmate could not say another negative word. I had shut the lion's mouth! Glory, hallelujah!

Later that day as I was driving home, my thoughts were on my classmate and the conversation we had earlier. Realizing that I had been just like her, some years prior, I understood that my frustration was not with her but the spirit that motivated her. As I thought back on my earlier years, I remembered, how I had such a negative attitude. I would sabotage my own life with such a negative attitude. I did not believe anything I did would work. In addition to sabotaging my life, I would do it to family and friends by speaking negatively and unbelief in their lives. Before I met Jesus, I was full of negativity and unbelief.

When I began attending church learning and applying the principles of Christ to my life, my perspective on life itself begin to change. As I continued to listen to Bishop Grannum, of the New Covenant Church in Philadelphia teach from the Bible, as I continued to read, pray, and live by the Word of God, and as I continued to fellowship with the people of God, I began to learn and grow in the ways of God. I also began to learn more of who God is, what he expects, and who I am in Him.

As I grew spiritually, I began to wonder about the plight of the church. It seemed paradoxical to me that if she (the church) has the same kind of power that Jesus has then what is wrong? I soon realized that some saints, it appeared, were walking in unbelief. I say this because there are people who attend church every Sunday, claiming to know God, yet they are so negative that they refuse to believe God's word or even speak the word over their lives. I have met many people in the church who do not believe God. They do not say it but it is in the very words they speak and the actions they exemplify. They just do not have faith in God or His Word. It is my hope that after you read this chapter, you will be able to recognize an unbelieving heart, whether it is your own or someone else's. Then, I will discuss how an unbelieving heart can be changed.

As I discussed in my previous book *10 Things God Expects*, "unbelief will block the blessings of God from flowing in your life." In the biblical context, unbelief means faithlessness or disbelief. It is the total opposite of faith. The word is used only five times in the gospels and Jesus only taught on it once in Matthew 17:14-18. When Jesus appointed His disciples to go forth two by two, He gave them power over unclean spirits. Unfortunately, the disciples were unable to cure a certain child. The child's father went to Jesus seeking healing for his son. He told Jesus that the disciples were unable to cure the boy. Then Jesus answered and said, "**O faithless** and perverse generation, how long shall I be with you? How long shall I suffer you?" Jesus rebuked the devil, cured the child, and then told the disciples they were operating with **NO** faith. Oddly, the disciples were perplexed that they were unable to heal the man's son. Additionally, they believed they had enough faith to cast out the demon that held the boy captive. They were unaware that they lacked faith because they asked the question: "Why could we not cast him out?" And Jesus said unto them, Because of your **unbelief** . . ." (Matthew 17:18-20a). Jesus was saying to His disciples, even though you spoke the word of God and rebuked the devil, you did not really believe in your heart this thing you spoke would come to pass. Jesus did not say because you had just a little bit of belief. He told the disciples they did not have **any** belief in what they were saying or doing. Jesus then continued and said: "For verily I say unto you, If ye have faith as a grain of mustard seed, ye shall say unto this mountain, remove hence to yonder place; and it shall remove; and nothing shall be impossible unto you" (Matthew 17:20b). Next, Jesus proceeded to tell them how they could be set free from this kind of unbelief. "Howbeit this kind goeth not out but by prayer and fasting" (Matthew 17:21). I used to believe Jesus was talking about the kind of demon, which possessed the boy would go out by prayer and fasting. Jesus was not talking about the boy, but he was talking about the kind of deep-seated, deceptive unbelief the disciples harbored in their hearts. It is the depth of this spirit that will only be destroyed by prayer and fasting.

Unbelief is very deceiving because it is able to hide behind religion. A person with unbelief will say that miracles do not happen today. When God does a miracle in someone's life, the unbeliever will explain it away scientifically or by saying, "I know God is able but . . ." They will also say, "whatever is God's will." They do not really understand that His word is His will. Subsequently, if they knew his word they would know that all things are possible because the Bible says, "With God all things are possible" (Matthew 19:26). They would also know that Jesus died so that we could have life more abundantly (John 10:10). They would understand that if we ask anything of Jesus, He will give it to us (John 14:14). They would understand that if we have faith as a grain of mustard seed, we can speak to any situation or circumstance we find ourselves in and we would overcome (Matthew 17:20). They would understand that healing is the children's bread and that God sent His Word (Jesus) to heal us and to deliver us from all infirmities so we would use His word to receive our healing (Psalm 107:20; Matthew 8:16; Luke 7:7).

An unbelieving heart will also pray for self and others and believes in his heart that nothing will happen and then will justify it by saying, "some things are just not meant to be." Several years ago, I hosted my own Christian radio broadcast. Every night before the show went off the air, I would encourage my listeners to call in for prayer. When they did, I would pray for the people of God and was certain in my heart God would heal them. Some would even call back to give me a praise report of their healing. Through this ministry, thank God, many people were delivered and set free from all types of sicknesses and diseases. One night after the show, a gentleman called and wanted me to pray that Christ would open his blind eyes. However, when this man who, wanted not just a miracle, but, (as I saw it), a supernatural miracle, I did not believe it would happen. Oh, yea, I prayed for him, but in my heart, there was unbelief. I was aware, at that moment in my heart, that I did not really believe God could do that particular miracle. After I prayed with him and finished the call, I began to pray to God that He would help my unbelief. Before this blind man called, I believed I had faith for anything, but I did not. This is the state of the body of Christ today. We say we believe God, and His Word, but do we really?

I suppose, in the body of Christ many pastors and laymen are operating in unbelief which is why there is a lack of God's power being manifested in the church. One well-known Christian said while in seminary that as he examined the claims of Christian faith he could not accept it. As he continued to search the scriptures with an open heart, he found the Lord. Dear reader, I invite you to begin by reading and begin to follow Jesus' teachings. Try to put, as best you can, his words he taught in action. Begin to talk with the Lord and tell him your shortcomings. Eventually, He will reveal Himself to you and your heart of unbelief will turn into a repentant heart one that seeks after God.

To change a heart of unbelief, one must believe on the Son of God. Jesus said, "This is the work of God that ye believe on him whom he hath sent" (John 6:29). In order to believe God and receive power and authority from God, one must believe He exist and have faith in Him. The writer of Hebrews puts it this way, "But without faith it is impossible to please him: for he that cometh to God must believe that he is, and that he is a rewarder of them that diligently seek him" (Hebrews 11:6). When you seek God, he will be found of you. Jeremiah declares, "Then shall ye call upon me, and ye shall go and pray unto me, and I will hearken unto you. And ye shall seek me, and find me, when ye shall search for me with all your heart. And I will be found of you, saith the LORD . . ." (29:12-14a). When you have faith in God and seek after God, He will reveal more of Himself to you and then reward you for seeking after Him. There were many that did not believe the Word of God, but sought after him and found he is a God who will reveal himself to those who seek him. God says if you seek me you will find me (Deuteronomy 4:29). He wants to dispel your unbelief because unbelief will hinder you from entering into the promises of God (Hebrews 3:1).

Finally, the unbelieving heart can be changed by reading and studying the Word of God. In His word, He will reveal His truths to you. When you continue to read and study his word, God will give you the "spirit of wisdom and revelation in the knowledge of Him" that only he can give. (Ephesians 1:17). God said, "This book of the law shall not depart out of thy mouth; but thou shall meditate therein day and night . . ." (Joshua 1:8). The psalmist wrote that we ought to, "mediate day and night in his law" (Psalm 1:1-3). Jesus said, "Man should not live by bread alone, but by every word that proceedeth out of the mouth of God." It is the desire of our heavenly Father that the unbelieving heart would change, believe Him and repent.

Chapter Six

AN EVIL HEART

**And God saw that the wickedness of man was great in the earth,
and that every imagination of the thoughts of his heart was
only evil continually.**

Osama bin Laden, Jeffery Dahmer, the Reverend Jim Jones, Idi Amin, Adolf Hitler, 9/11, The Holocaust, and Slavery in America provoke gruesome images for those who remember the influences these people and events had on society. These names and events may stir up a range of emotions as they may also conjure up devastating images in the mind relationally. Many of us, if not all, will cringe or even shed tears when we view the images of the devastation. And many of us, if not all, will agree that evil can be associated with these names and events. The dictionary defines *evil* as "morally reprehensible, wicked, and sinful. It arises from actual or imputed bad character or conduct." In view of this definition, we can say that the conduct of a man defines his character. In other words, it is in his works, words, and deeds that will ultimately show whether he is of good character or evil character and whether his heart is good or evil. In this chapter, I will look at a couple of stories that reveal the evil hearts of men, I will also share information on what God says about an evil heart, and then answer the question: can an evil heart repent and be changed?

The first time the word "evil" is recorded in the Bible, it is found in Genesis 6:5: "And God saw that the wickedness of man was great in the earth, and that every imagination of the thoughts of his heart was only evil continually." The Bible says, God was so grieved in His heart that He was sorry He had made man on the earth so He said, "I will destroy man whom I have created from the face of the earth . . ." (Genesis 6:6-7). Previously, in the same chapter, we read that the daughters that were born of men were "fair" and the "sons of God" took them as wives and they bare children to them and they became "mighty men." There are many who believe the "sons of God" were fallen angels that had sex with women.

Although there was much wickedness in the earth, there was one man amongst all the evil in the world who was "a just man" and the Bible said, "Noah walked with God" (Genesis 6:9). Noah was a descendent of Adam (see genealogy in Genesis 5) who had three sons Shem, Ham, and Japheth. When God looked upon the earth he saw that all flesh was corrupt and he said to Noah, "The end of all flesh is come before me; for the earth is filled with violence through them, and behold; I will destroy them with the earth" (Genesis 6:13). Then God instructed Noah to make an ark, and he gave him, specific measurements of the length, the breadth, and the height of it (Genesis 6:15). He also told Noah, how he was going to destroy the earth saying, "and behold, I even I, do bring a flood of waters upon the earth, to destroy all flesh, wherein is the breath of life, from under heaven; and everything that is in the earth shall die" (Genesis 6:17). God then told Noah what to do after he built the Ark. "Come thou and thy house into the ark . . . for I have seen that you are righteous before me in this generation" (Genesis 7:1; The New English Version). I have heard many who said they do not believe the story of the flood in the Bible. All they need to do is look around and see how the Tsunamis of today are destroying whole cities.

Noah was righteous and obedient to God while surrounded by an evil environment. How was he able to walk in submission to the Lord with such wickedness all around him? Probably because of the word he heard about God from his father which was passed down from generation to generation. This is the reason we ought to teach our children God's word so they will be able to stand when confronted with evil. As a matter fact, the Lord instructs us to teach the children his laws and his commandments:

> Ye shall **teach** them your **children**, speaking of them when thou sittest in thine house and when thou walkest by the way, when thou liest down, and when thou risest up (Deuteronomy 11:18-19).

Our God has given us the peace to stand while evil is raging all around us and to be unaffected by it. He has equipped us with his armor, which is our protective covering. This armor includes His written Word and the power and authority of His Holy Spirit living within us. God is able to keep us from falling because greater is he that is in us than he that is in the world (1 John 4:4). Just as Noah was righteous and obedient to God during a period of extreme wickedness, we can be also. We must be willing to seek God and call on Him for His strength, goodness and grace.

After the ark was complete, Noah, his wife, their three sons and their sons' wives, entered into the ark with the required number of animals as God instructed male and female.

> And, behold, I even I, do bring a flood of waters upon the earth, to destroy all flesh, wherein is the breath of life, from under heaven; and everything that is in the earth shall die. But with thee will I establish my covenant; and thou shalt come into the ark, thou, and thy sons, and thy wife, and thy sons wives with thee. And of every living thing of all flesh, two of every sort shalt thou bring into the ark, to keep them alive with thee, they shall be male and female . . . And take thou unto thee of all food that is eaten . . . and it shall be for food for thee, and for them. Thus did Noah; according to all that God commanded him so did he (Genesis 6:17-22).

The Bible says then the Lord "shut him in the ark" and it began to rain. It rained for forty days and destroyed every living thing on the face of the earth. After the flood, Noah built an altar unto the Lord . . . And the Lord smelled a sweet savour . . . and God blessed Noah and his sons, and said unto them, "be fruitful, and multiply, and replenish the earth. And Noah lived after the flood 350 years" (Genesis 9:28-29). From this account, we see the judgment of God came upon all flesh because of the corruption, violence, wickedness, and evilness in the hearts of men.

Another place in the Bible where the conduct and character of men reveal their evil hearts is in Genesis 19, in the story of Sodom and

Gomorrah. This was a place where wickedness prevailed mightily and where the Lord condemned all but one family.

"And there came two angels to Sodom at even and Lot sat in the gate of Sodom" (Genesis 19:1).

Lot was Abram's nephew and because of the strife between their herdsmen they agreed to separate (Genesis 11:31; 12:5). "And Abram said unto Lot, Let there be no strife, I pray thee, between me and thee, and between my herdsmen and thy herdsmen, for we be brethren. Is not the whole land before thee? Separate thyself, I pray thee, from me: if thou wilt take the left hand, then I will go to the right: or if thou depart to the right hand, then I will go to the left" (Genesis 13:8-9). Abram told Lot, whichever direction you decide to go, I will take the opposite. "Seeing the land was well watered," Lot went into Sodom and Gomorrah and dwelled there. How long he was there before the Lord decided to destroy the land, the Bible does not say. What it does say is that in Sodom and Gomorrah "the men of Sodom were and sinners before the Lord exceedingly" (Genesis 13:13). A couple of things I want to point out. Although Abram walked by faith, while his nephew Lot did not. Lot made his decisions by sight and walked right into a sinful and wicked environment. This tells us that we should not go by how things look because although it may look good, it may hurt or harm our walk with the Lord. There is an old cliché that says, "all that glitters is not gold." The Bible clearly states we should walk by faith and not by sight. Always seek God for direction to avoid the snares and traps of the enemy.

Lot may have been better off staying in Haran the land of his childhood. The Lord never called him out of Haran. The call was for Abram and his family. The "Lord had said unto Abram; Get thee out of thy country, and from thy kindred, and from thy father's house . . ." Then we read, "So Abram departed, as the Lord had spoken unto him; and Lot went with him . . ." (Genesis 12:1 & 4). Abram no doubt welcomed Lot to come along because he was family and he was probably comfortable, like many of us, with family being around. But God often times calls us away from family to set us apart for himself. The lesson here is to always seek God to order your footsteps and show you the direction to go. Listen to wise counsel; it is fantastic and is worth its weight in gold. And make sure you have peace in your heart concerning the matter. God may call you to go in a totally different direction than he had your sister, brother, mother, or father to pursue. Always seek God for yourself.

It is interesting to note that the Lord did not give Abram any further instructions on his journey until Lot was separated from him. The Bible states, "the Lord said unto Abram, AFTER . . . LOT WAS SEPARATED FROM HIM, Lift up now thine eyes, and look from the place where thou art northward, and southward, and eastward, and westward; For all the land which thou seest, to thee will I give it, and to thy seed forever" (Genesis 13:14). The relationship with Abram and Lot shows us that there are times your greater blessings, anointing, and power cannot be received until you come out of a wrong relationship.

Another account given in the Bible where evil dwelt in the hearts of men was Sodom and Gomorrah. Sodom and Gomorrah were a part of a larger agricultural confederation of five cities known as the Cities of the Plain, which included Zoar, Admah, and Zeboim. Zoar, the city where Lot and his two daughters ran, after being led out of Sodom, was the only city not destroyed by fire (Genesis 18:22). According to the Bible, the sin of those regions were over indulgence in food (Ezekiel 16:49), adultery, lying tongue, evildoers (Jeremiah 23:14), and homosexuality (Genesis 19:4-7). And the Lord said, because the cry of Sodom and Gomorrah is great and because their sin is very grievous; I will go down [there] now . . . (Genesis 18:20-21).

Genesis 19:1 records the two angels went into Sodom. When they arrived, they saw Lot sitting at the gate of Sodom (This was a large area where the people would gather for community business and for meeting with friends). When Lot saw them, he invited them to stay with him, when they refused, "he pressed upon them greatly; and they turned unto him, and entered into his house." (Lot was being hospitable as was the custom of the day. He also knew the dangers that were on the streets at night). He then made them a feast and they sat and ate.

> But before they lay down, the men of the city, even the men of Sodom, compassed the house round, both old and young, all the people from every quarter: And they called unto Lot, and said unto him, where are the men who came in to thee this night? Bring them out unto us, that we may know them. And Lot went out at the door unto them, and shut the door after him, And said, I pray you, brethren, do not so wickedly. (Genesis 19:4-7)

What evilness lurked in the hearts of these men! The Bible tells us these men were young and old men of Sodom that was at Lot's door.

This is an example of the sins of the fathers being passed down from generation to generation. (Exodus 20:5) Although the commandments had not been given or written yet, Lot sees this act as wicked. Paul, in the book of Romans addresses this saying,

For when the Gentiles, which have not the law, do by nature the things contained in the law, these, having not the law, are a law unto themselves: Which shew the work of the law written in their hearts, their conscience also bearing witness, and their thoughts the mean while accusing or else excusing one another . . . (Romans 2:14-15)

Lot's conscience bare him witness of what was right and wrong. The moral decay of the other inhabitants of Sodom, however, appeared not to have affected Lot to such a degree. Probably because Lot saw his uncle praying to God and seeing prayers answered. That is why it is so important to pray with our children. I am sure his uncle told him about all his encounters with the Lord. Abram, must have certainly told him of all that he knew of the Almighty God who made the heavens and the earth because in the scriptures we read that He commanded and trained his household in the ways of God (Genesis 18:19). And he was sure to have told Lot about the accounts he had heard his father and grandfather talk about regarding the tower of Babel. And of course he would have told him what he heard of Noah and the building of the Ark along with the creation story and the account of Cain slaying his brother Abel. Lot's faith was probably strengthened in the Lord because of the stories he heard from his uncle.

Dear reader, do you encourage your children, family, and friends of the great things God has done for you? It is important for us to tell our children and others the miracles God has done for us so their faith can be strengthened in the Lord. Most certainly, Abram's story and lifestyle had to have had some influence on Lot. It was no doubt Lot was rooted and grounded in the ways, works, and word of God. Perhaps he thought homosexuality was an abomination and a lesser crime than the gang-rape of his daughters. Maybe that is why he said, "Behold now, I have two daughters which have not known man; let me, I pray you, bring them out unto you and do ye to them as is good in your eyes . . ." Genesis 19:8). Additionally, Lot probably saw his daughters as his property, which was how women were seen in biblical times, belonging either to their father or to their husband. Therefore, Lot probably believed it was his right to offer his property to the sinful mob and have his daughters suffer shame;

rather than turn the angels, who were guest in his house, over to the men of Sodom.

In addition to observing Abram's godly lifestyle, Lot must have examined how Abram treated his wife. He would have learned how to treat the women in his life by what he heard and saw in his uncle's house. Unfortunately, many young men today do not have godly examples of how to treat women during their youth. This is one reason why we see and hear such blatant disrespect towards girls and young ladies in music, movies and television shows. Lot was there when Abram and his family went into Egypt because of the famine that was in the land. He was also there when Abram told his beautiful wife, Sarai, to lie and say she was his sister instead of his wife. Lot had seen the manipulation and the conniving spirit of his uncle because of fear. Lot observed how Abram used his wife to save his own life.

> And it came to pass, when he was come near to enter into Egypt, that he said unto Sarai his wife, Behold now, I know that thou art a fair woman to look upon . . . when the Egyptians shall see thee, that they shall say, This is his wife: and they will kill me. But they will save thee alive. Say, I pray thee, thou art my sister. (Genesis 11-13).

And Lot was there to see the hand of the Lord against Pharaoh and his entire house because of Sari who had been taken into Pharaoh's house.

"And the Lord plagued Pharaoh and his house with great plagues because of Sarai Abram's wife. And Pharaoh called Abram, and said, "What is this that thou hast done unto me? Why didst thou not tell me that she was thy wife? Why saidist thou, she is my sister? So I might have taken her to me to wife: now therefore behold thy wife, take her, and go thy way" (Genesis 12:17-19).

Perhaps Lot thought the Lord would rescue his daughters as He had rescued Sarai. If this was how he was thinking, he was right. Unbeknownst to him, he had two angels in his house. The book of Hebrews tells us to "be not forgetful to entertain strangers: for thereby some have entertained angels unawares" (Hebrews 13:2). So when the men of Sodom refused his daughters, they said to Lot: Are you a judge? "Stand back . . . now [or] we deal worse with thee, than with them" (Genesis 19:9). The men begin to press up against Lot at which point the angels, put forth their hands and pulled him into the house and shut the door. Then they "Smote the men that were at the door of the house with blindness" so they could not find the door (Genesis 19:10-11). They then revealed to Lot who they were and told Lot they were sent by the Lord to bring them out and to destroy the city. Lot told his family but his sons-in-law thought he was joking. I am curious as to where Lot's sons-in-law were when Lot offered his daughters to the mob. Nevertheless, they did not believe Lot when he told them of the judgment of God. The next morning, the angels told Lot to take his wife and his two daughters and leave the city.

And "while he lingered, the men [angels] laid hold upon his hand and upon the hand of his wife, and upon the hand of his two daughters; the Lord being merciful unto him and they brought him forth, and set him without the city" (Genesis 19:16).

The angels told Lot to flee and: "escape for thy life; look not behind thee, neither stay thou in all the plain, escape to the mountain." Unfortunately, Lot still did not trust the Lord, and still was unable to walk by faith. Lot responded, "I cannot escape to the mountain, lest some evil take me, and I die." His fear and lack of faith convinced him that the Lord would save him from the judgment of Sodom to be overtaken by evil in the mountain and die. Lot insisted that he would be safer in a nearby city, Zoar; so the angels agreed and as they were fleeing for their lives, Lot's wife looked back and was destroyed.

What can we learn as we look at the lives of Lot and those surrounding him? First, let us look at Lot's wife. She is mentioned three times in the Scriptures (Genesis 19:16; 19:26; Luke 17:31-33). During troubling times and in the time of urgency, she had difficulty obeying the word of the Lord. She lingered and the angel had to grab a hold of her hand to get her out of the city. And even when it looked as if she was safe, she perished. Some churchgoers think they are safe from eternal damnation just because they are a member of a particular church. They come to church faithfully, work in the ministry, and say praise the Lord while the pastor preaches but still they are in danger of hell's fire. They have never accepted Jesus as their personal Savior. They walk in disobedience and never give it a second thought. Sure, they have a relationship with the pastor and the saints of God, but they never establish a relationship with Jesus Christ the Son of the living God. Jesus said, the son of man must be lifted up; "that whosoever believeth in him should not perish, but have eternal life. For God so loved the world, that he gave his only begotten Son, that whosoever believeth in him should not perish, but have everlasting life. For God sent not his Son into the world to condemn the world; but that the world through him might be saved. He that believeth on him is not condemned; but he that believeth not is condemned already, because he hath not believed in the name of the only begotten Son of God. (John 3:3; 3:15-18). Additionally, Lot's wife disobeyed the instructions of the angels. Lot and his family were told to escape to the mountain and do not look back. Perhaps she walked in disobedience because Lot walked in disobedience. Lot was given an order by the angels to go into the mountain. Lot believed he would die in the mountain. Can you imagine that? God just delivered him from Sodom, and Lot believes he is being sent up into the mountain to die. Maybe if Lot had obeyed God, perhaps his wife would have obeyed him. Husbands, when you disobey God, it leaves the door open for the enemy to trick your wife and children. Another thing we can learn from Lot's wife. She looked back. Why did she look back? She may have been looking back at her past. When the Lord sets us free from the bondage of sin, we should not look back. And the enemy uses our past to hinder us from moving into our destiny. When we are set free from the hurts, pains, and bruises of the past, we should not look back. The enemy uses our hurts, pains, and bruises to keep us in unforgiveness. In order to be forgiven of your trespasses and sins, you must forgive others (Matthew 6:12-16). Jesus said forgive those who trespass against you because when we forgive others, our heavenly Father will forgive us. When the broken dreams, broken promises, and disappointments of the past have you in a state of sorrow, do not look back. The enemy uses these things to block your blessings. Jesus said, let not your heart be troubled . . . cast your cares (and concerns) on me . . . and I will give you rest (Matthew 11:28-30; John 14:1; John 14:27; 1 Peter 5:7). The past will hinder us from growing in the love of God and pull us away from the center of God's will for our lives. Another thing Lot's wife may have been concerned with was the possessions and people she left behind. As long as we love, covet, and identify with the things of this world and the people in our past, we will find it difficult to let go or move on when God calls us out.

Secondly, take a look at Lot's sons-in-law who thought Lot was joking about the impending doom. Most certainly Lot told them what happened to the young and old men of the city and how the angels struck them with blindness. They, like many in the world today, probably thought that the miracles of God are just coincidences. Moreover, when Lot told them of the judgment of God that would come upon the city they could not embrace it because there was something in their hearts that prevented the acceptance of this word from God. This is the attitude that many in the world have today about God's judgment in the earth, end-time prophecies, and eternal damnation for Satan and all his followers. They too think it is a joke and it does not pertain to them. They believe God's judgment and end-time prophecies will never happen. But they are wrong. Just as in the days of Noah and Lot they will enjoy eating, drinking, and their sinful life. Jesus makes this point during his ministry saying:

And as it was in the days of Noah, so shall it be also in the days of the Son of man. They did eat, they drank, they married wives, they were given in marriage, until the day that Noah entered into the ark, and the flood came, and destroyed them all. Likewise also as it was in the days of Lot; they did eat, they drank, they bought, they sold, they planted, they builded; but the same day that Lot went out of Sodom it rained fire and brimstone from heaven, and destroyed them all. Even thus shall it be in the days when the Son of man is revealed . . . (Luke 17:26-30).

Finally, let us look at Lot's life. We already know Lot did not fully walk in obedience to God. But why did Lot struggle with disobedience? We know at some level he believed God because he comes against the evilness of homosexuality. A closer look will reveal that Lot was a man of fear. We see Lot lingering in the house why, perhaps there was a fear of the unknown. Perhaps, lot was afraid to move forward into the future because he does not know the outcome. But he knows the outcome if he stays in Sodom. Dear reader, can you relate to being in a spot where you know you are being unproductive but you are afraid to move forward. You are afraid to try something new for the fear that engulfs you. Stop and trust God. Now that Lot is older, maybe he is tired of trying anything new. He realizes destruction will come to the city because he warns his sons-in-law. Yet he still lingers. One of the ways the devil hinders us is to try and paralyze us with fear. Then Lot verbally expresses his fear. When the angels told him to escape to the mountain, Lot said, he may be consumed or destroyed there. Look at Lot's rationale. He knows the angels are from God, he knows that God will destroy the city, he knows that he and his family are being spared from that city, and when he is given instructions on where to go, he believes in his heart that he will be destroyed in that place. Why would Lot think that God would spare him in one place to send him to another place to be destroyed? Saints of God, have you ever been given instructions by God and fear gripped you so deeply that you wanted to do something different or go in a different direction. Fear comes from the enemy; God says "Fear not." God says, "I have not given you the spirit of fear . . ." God says,: be not afraid, for I am with you and I will never leave you nor forsake you." If you are gripped with fear, dear heart, then pray and ask God to give you his peace. God loves you so much that he will give you his best. He delights and desires to give you His best, and He wants to lead you and guide you into your best life ever. The evil that surrounds you he will not let it hurt you nor will it harm you.

To conclude, evil was in the earth during the time of Noah. Evil was in the earth during the time of Lot. And Evil is in the earth today. But God can and will deliver us from evil as He promised he would in his word. He said, "if you call upon me I will answer you and show you my great salvation" (Psalm 86:7 & 91:15). God loves his creation so much that he sent Jesus to die for us (John 3:16-17). God realizes that evil lurks in the heart of every man, and that is why he sent his son, Jesus, to set us free from the bondage of evil. It was man's wicked ways that separated him from communing with God and man's wicked ways that condemns him to a life of eternal damnation. Jesus said that, ". . . an evil man out of the evil treasures [of his heart] bringeth forth evil things" (Matthew 12:35). Jeremiah said, "the heart is deceitful above all things; and disparately wicked who can know it?" (Jeremiah 17:9). Jesus said in Matthew 15:19," for out of the heart proceed evil thoughts, murders, adulteries, fornications, thefts, false witness, blasphemies . . ." The gospel of Mark adds to this list saying, "covetousness, wickedness, deceit, lasciviousness: an evil eye, blasphemy, pride, foolishness: all these evil things come from within," said Jesus, "and defile the man." These evil things line-up with the works of the flesh Paul talks about in Galatians 5:19-21. The writer of Hebrews adds one more point by labeling unbelief as evil (Hebrews 3:12) The Lord says," put away evil from thy flesh . . . [and] remember now thy creator . . ." (Ecclesiastes 11:102-12:1-3). God has given us a way out of our evilness, wickedness, and wretchedness, His Son, Jesus, and all we have to do is call on His name and repent.

Chapter Seven

A HARDENED HEART

"Today if ye will hear his voice, harden not your hearts"
(Hebrews 4:7)

The human heart is about the size of an individual's fist and it is the most essential organ in the human body. It is an important muscle because when it ceases to function death occurs within a matter of minutes. Its purpose is to pump blood to all parts of the body. The blood then delivers oxygen and nutrients to the cells in the human system. Our blood flows in one side of the heart and out the other side. With much information that we have about the heart in the United States, it is ironic that heart disease is 'the single leading cause of death. In the heart, glitches can occur, and a number of things can go wrong such as, clogged arteries, failure of the heart muscles and diseases. The problem may be the blood or the heart muscle. The causes of heart diseases some doctors say is that sometimes the problem is with the blood and sometimes it can be in the heart muscle. Some causes of heart diseases are high blood pressure, sugar diabetes, high cholesterol, rheumatic fever, atherosclerosis, and strokes.

Emotions are being linked to a host of heart diseases as well such as the ones mentioned above. Certain emotions can trigger hormones that can develop diseases. Also how a person feels emotionally can determine how they feel physically. Emotions can affect the heart and in turn can cause diseases that may damage the heart and destroy a person's life. When there is a considerable amount of stress a person is under, its believed it could lead to stroke, heart attack, or death.

There are emotions that are very harmful and detrimental to our bodies. The emotions that are harmful and most damaging are grief, guilt worry, fear, rage, unforgiveness, depression, anger. If continually intense, these emotions can harden arteries and become life threaten or deadly. These damaging and harmful emotions the Bible calls sin. In the same way these emotions are damaging to the body, if not addressed, these sinful emotions in the heart can be as equally damaging to the spirit. These emotions can cause one to lose faith in God and turn a deaf ear to his commandments. As these emotions continue to fester in the heart, the heart becomes harden. This will then lead to spiritual death and if repentance does not take place, possibly eternal damnation. In this chapter, we will look at several ways men harden their hearts against God's commandments and what are the consequences to a heart that is hardened against the Word of God.

Often times when we grow up under our parents, we tend to do some of the same things they did without giving a second thought of why we do them after we become an adult. Many of these things have been past down from generation to generation. They are called traditions. The dictionary's definition of tradition is, "an inherited, established, or customary pattern of thought, action, or behavior: as a religious practice or a social custom," for instance, exchanging cards and gifts for Valentine's Day, placing gifts under the Christmas Tree, and dying eggs for the Easter Bunny. These are all United States holidays and many of us do them because they have always been done that way. If someone comes along who does not follow the tradition or talk against it or insists you are in error, how difficult would it be to discontinue your tradition? Would you fight to the death to continue what you have always done, whether it's right or wrong? Traditions of men are one way many may blind their eyes and harden their heart to the truth in God's Word. This is what was happening during Jesus' time. The people were firm in their traditions and very rigid in making sure things were done the way it's always been done. Many of the religious practices that were done were not of God. They were established by men, mostly the religious leaders, and followed by God's people without questioning them. They believed they were following and worshiping God. When Jesus came, He revealed the truth about traditions. The religious leaders such as the Scribes, in that day, were very pious in giving the law, while adding rules onto the law and pretending to live by the law. In Matthew 15:2, they asked Jesus why the disciples **transgress the tradition of the elders** and Jesus replied:

> . . . why do ye also **transgress the commandment of God by your tradition**? For God commanded, saying, Honor thy father and mother and, He that curseth father or mother, let him die the death. But ye say . . . he shall be free. Thus have ye made the commandment of God of none effect by your tradition (Matthew 15:2-6).

How surprised they must have been that Jesus asked them this question. They were the leaders that copied, read, and interpreted the Law. And they were also the men the people would go to for godly wisdom, understanding, and insight. Jesus then calls them hypocrites saying:

Ye hypocrites, well did Esaias prophesy of you, saying, This people draweth nigh unto me with their mouth, and honoureth me with their lips but their heart is far from me . . . (Matthew 15:7-8)

When Jesus came on the scene with his message of repentance and the kingdom of God, the Scribes were against His teachings and they hardened their hearts toward His message. People of God, if we are in a church where the man and woman of God are hearing from and honoring God with their whole heart, we must be very careful not to harden our hearts when we hear the Word of God. When Jesus healed a man who was sick of the palsy, Scribes and Pharisees hardened their heart and called him a blasphemer in Matthew 9:1-3. They were displeased with Jesus when they saw "the wonderful things that he had done and the children crying . . . Hosanna to the son of David" (Matthew 21:15). After seeing how He healed many, how the unclean spirits fell down at Jesus' feet calling Him the Son of God, and seeing the crowds follow and want to touch him the Scribes said, "He hath *Beelzebub*, and by the prince of the devils casteth he out devils" (Matthew 12:22-28). But Jesus called them unto him and said unto them, "how can Satan cast out Satan? And if a kingdom be divided against itself that kingdom cannot stand" (Matthew 3:26; Mark 12:26). In other words Jesus was saying if Satan is holding these people in bondage with their diseases, illnesses, and infirmities, and then he heals them, how can his kingdom survive? If Satan releases people from drugs, alcohol, lying, cheating, stealing, homosexuality, bestiality, pornography, molestation, fornication, adultery, greed, pride, theft, backbiting, killing, murders, and all other sinful thoughts and acts, how will his kingdom ever stand? Jesus points out how ridiculous and senseless are their accusations. He also wanted to let them know how hardened their hearts are to the truth and then he warns them:

Verily I say unto you, all sins shall be forgiven unto the sons of men, and blasphemies whatsoever they shall blaspheme: But he that shall blaspheme against the Holy Ghost hath never forgiveness, but is in danger of eternal damnation:

Jesus was letting them know what I do, I do by the Holy Spirit that dwells in me. You are not denying the miracles I perform, but you are denying the power of the Holy Ghost and then saying God's work is the work of Satan. This is a sin that will not be forgiven.

Dear reader, we should be careful in our own lives not to falsely accuse someone who is Spirit filled, and be sure not to harden our heart to curse, swear, or speak against the Holy Ghost that lives within them. The Scribes not only accused him of having a devil they questioned him, (Mark 2:16; Mark 12:28); they provoked him, (Luke 11:53); they rejected him, (Mark 8:31); they mocked him (Mark 15:31); they assembled together to destroy him (Matthew 26:3; Luke 19:47; 22:2); they accused him (Mark 15:1); and they killed him (Mark 14:1). The hearts of the Scribes were so harden by their traditions that they would rather kill than to change. Be careful not to harden your hearts to the word and the spirit of God like the Scribes. When you hear the word of God and the voice of God, be willing to open your heart and accept him into your life.

The Pharisees, because of their traditions, were another group of religious folks that hardened their hearts to Jesus' message. The name *Pharisee* in its Hebrew form means "separatists or the separated ones." They were also known as *chasidim,* in Hebrew, which means "loyal to or loved of God"—extremely ironic in view of the fact they made themselves the most bitter, and deadly, opponents of Jesus Christ and His message.

"Then came together unto him the Pharisees, and certain of the scribes, which came from Jerusalem. And when they saw some of his disciples eat bread with defiled, that is to say, with unwashen, hands, they found fault. For the Pharisees, and all the Jews, except they wash their hands oft, eat not, holding the tradition of the elders . . . Then the

Pharisees and scribes asked him, why walk not thy disciples according to the tradition of the elders, but eat bread with unwashen hands" (Mark 7:1-3 & 5)?

Here we read that the Pharisees and all the Jews did not eat unless they wash their hands often. Now this tradition was passed down from generation to generation. We read in Leviticus 6, the priests were instructed to wash themselves and all instruments while serving before the Lord in the temple. This was only an act of cleanliness and had nothing to do with the heart. But now we read during Jesus' time, this tradition is for everyone. And it is believed that if it is done, it honors God. Jesus said, in vain you call yourselves worshiping me by washing the outside while the inside (your heart) is still harden toward the Father. Jesus knew the manner in which it was being done was hypocritical. So He answers them saying:

Well hath Esaias prophesied of you hypocrites, as it is written, this people honoureth me with their lips, but their heart is far from me. Howbeit in vain do they worship me, teaching for doctrines the commandments of men. (Mark 7:6-7).

Jesus quoting Isaiah said to the Pharisees, you are praying but just moving your lips. Your heart is not even focused on God. Saints of God, are there traditions set up by men in your church that have nothing to do with worshiping God? Are these things mandated by your leaders for you to do in honor to God? If a stranger came into your church, full of God's Spirit and Word, would he be able to say the same things Jesus said to the Scribes and Pharisees? How would he be received with honor or dishonor? Listen to what Jesus said to the Scribes and Pharisees:

But woe unto you, Scribes and Pharisees, hypocrites! For ye shut up the kingdom of heaven against men: for ye neither go in yourselves, neither suffer ye them that are entering to go in (Matthew 23:13).

Woe unto you, scribes and Pharisees, hypocrites! for ye compass sea and land to make one proselyte, and when he is made, ye make him twofold more the child of hell than yourselves. Woe unto you, ye blind guides . . . (Matthew 23:15-16).

Woe unto you, scribes and Pharisees, hypocrites! for ye make clean the outside of the cup and of the platter, but within they are full of extortion and excess. Thou blind Pharisee, cleanse first that which is within the cup and platter, that the outside of them may be clean also (Matthew 23:25-26).

Does this sound like some of God's people today? Good looking saints of God on the outside but full of sin and death in their harden hearts. You can tell by how they talk and how they live. They leave church on Sunday and live like hellions the rest of the week. They tell others about getting their life right but cannot seem to get their own life on track. Pastors, prophets, evangelists, and teachers preaching and teaching the Word of God yet doing everything they can do contrary to God's Word and then try to justify it.

For laying aside the commandment of God ye hold the tradition of men . . . ye reject the commandment of God, that ye may keep your own tradition. (Mark 7:8).

The Scribes and the Pharisees missed the blessings of God because of their traditions. They rejected the son of God because of their traditions. It was also because of their traditions that they did not hear and heed to the voice of God saying repent the kingdom of God is at hand.

Dear Reader, are you able to recognize your traditions that contradict the kingdom of God, the Word of God, and the Son of God. Apostle Paul was not able to recognize his traditions and his hardened heart toward Jesus the Christ. In his letter to the Galatians, Paul reminds them how zealous he was and blinded by tradition saying:

For ye have heard of my conversation in time past in the Jews' religion, how that beyond measure I persecuted the church of God, and wasted it: And profited in the Jews' religion above many my equals in mine own nation, being more exceedingly zealous of the traditions of my fathers (Galatians 1:13-14).

Paul believed that what he was doing was right while he was killing and persecuting Christians but the Bible states, "There is a way that seems right to man but the end thereof is the way of death" (Proverbs 14:12).

It is not only traditions that can harden the heart against the Word of God, but prejudiced views can also harden a man's heart to God's Word. Jesus tells a compelling story of the Good Samaritan, ". . . A certain man went down from Jerusalem to Jericho, and fell among thieves, which stripped him of his raiment, and wounded him, and departed, leaving him half dead" (Luke 10:30).

The road that connects Jerusalem to Jericho is seventeen miles long. It is a steep, winding and remote road that for centuries has been a place of robberies. We do not know the ethnicity of the victim who was attack, but we can only presume he was Jewish since Jesus himself was a Jew. Nevertheless, we see in this parable, the man being a typology of Christ, who was beaten, stripped of His raiment, hung, and left to die.

And by chance there came down a certain priest that way: and when he saw him, he passed by on the other side. (Luke 10:31)

Perhaps the priest passed on the other side initially because of fear. He may have thought the man that was lying on the road was a thief who was plotting and waiting for someone to assist him so that the thieves could then attack. Surely, when he was closer to the man, he saw that he was an injured victim. It may have been his prejudice views of the people on the Jericho road that blinded his judgment to assist and serve. How tragic it is to see a priest, one who is a mediator between man and God, ignore and show no mercy or compassion toward his brethren. Exodus 10:11 states that the priest, "may teach the children of Israel all the statutes which the LORD hath spoken unto them . . ." This priest taught on mercy, acts of kindness, and love. Yet this day, he could show none of these godly traits. It could very well have been his preconceived prejudicial impressions that clouded his judgment on this day when one of his brethren needed his assistance.

And likewise a Levite, when he was at the place, came and looked on him, and passed by on the other side. (Luke 10:32)

A Levite is presumed to be of the Hebrew tribe of Levi. When Moses was in Mt. Sinai getting the Ten Commandments, the Levites were the only tribe that stood for the Lord, while the other tribes were committing idolatry. Aaron and Moses belonged to this tribe and the tribe of Levi showed itself to be on the Lord's side at that time (Exodus 32:25-28). Also, when Joshua led the Israelites into the land of Canaan, the Levites were the only Israelite tribe who received cities but no tribal land because the Lord the God of Israel himself would be their inheritance (Joshua 13:33). They had not only religious responsibilities but political ones as well

(Numbers 1:49-51). Their roles in the temple included singing Psalms during temple services, performing construction, and maintenance for the temple, serving as guards, and other services.

The point Jesus was making is that the Levites also knew the Law and knew the instructions of God; they believed if a brethren was in need of assistance, it is your responsibility to help as a brother and as a Jewish leader. The Levite did more than the priest because he took a greater effort to see the dying man. Jesus said, he "came and looked on him" and then when he saw him, he "passed by on the other side." What did he see that made him ignore the victim? Did he see one who was of a different tribe, different religion, or perhaps a different ethnicity? Perhaps he thought it was not his problem. How could he justify leaving this wounded, helpless, dying man on this dismal road? Perhaps he thought the load of carrying the man would be too hard or heavy for him. Maybe he thought his family and friends would have thought him foolish to be of assistance to anyone on that dangerous highway. Whatever his reasoning, he went over to see the man, he looked at the man, and then he went on the other side to avoid helping the man. Many people today may think the load of carrying someone less fortunate may be too heavy. Others may think helping others of a different race or religion is inappropriate. And there are some who may not act on helping others because of what they believe their family and friends may say, i.e., they fear they may be ridiculed by their loved ones for helping strangers. But Jesus said, "Except your righteousness shall exceed the righteousness of the scribes and Pharisees, ye shall in no case enter into the kingdom of heaven" and "Let your light so shine before men, that they may see your good works, and glorify your Father which is in heaven" (Matthew 5:16 & 20).

But a certain Samaritan, as he journeyed, came where he was: and when he saw him, he had compassion on him (Luke 10:33).

Religiously, the Samaritans are a separate religion to Judaism. Based on the Samaritan Torah, Samaritans claim their worship is the true religion, while the Jews claimed they were the true worshippers of God. Nevertheless, Jesus was explaining to the people that God wanted a remnant that would follow mercy, truth, and love, as well as, the understanding who their Father is. Hosea puts it this way: "For I desired mercy, and not sacrifice: and the knowledge of God more than burnt sacrifice" (Hosea 6:6). The Good Samaritan showed great mercy he:

> . . . went to him, and bound up his wounds, pouring in oil and wine, and set him on his own beast, and brought him to an inn, and took care of him And on the morrow when he departed, he took out two pence, and gave them to the host, and said unto him, Take care of him; and whatsoever thou spendest more, when I come again, I will repay thee (Luke 10:34-35).

This man showed him love and compassion. Even though the victim may have appeared to be of a lesser economic status, a different religious background, and perhaps a different ethnicity, he still extended help. He spent his time, talent, and money on a complete stranger. The Samaritan did not let anything cloud his judgment on this issue. In his heart, he knew the right thing to do was to show mercy and extend a helping hand to his brethren even if his brother is different than he.

Today, Jesus is telling all of us to go and show the same kind of mercy and loving kindness to our fellow man. We have an obligation like the Good Samaritan to assist our neighbors in need whether that neighbor is next door or around the world. If your traditions or your prejudices are hindering you from obeying the Word of God and your heart is harden to God's word on mercy, love, and compassion then today is the day to repent.

Chapter Eight

A GRIEVED HEART

. . . why weepest thou? And why eatest thou not?
And why is thy heart grieved?
(1 Samuel 1:8)

During the course of any given day, the majority of us never give a thought about our mortality. We do not think about the loss, pain, hurt, mental anguish, or any emotions that come with death. But at the moment death occurs it leaves behind, in the heart, soul, and mind lingering moments, days, and years of grief. When it is an individual loss, it seems to be a period of time one is expected to grieve and then move on. While our loved ones and friends continue to change and grow, we become frozen in time, trapped in memory, loss, and grief. In this chapter, we will focus on two Biblical characters who faced grief and how they chose to address it.

In the previous chapter, you may recall that grief is one of the emotions that is damaging to the body. Exactly what is grief? It is defined in the *Dictionary* "as an intense emotional suffering caused by loss, disaster, and misfortune" and an "acute sorrow and deep sadness." Grief is a normal response to loss and is an emotion that is felt when something or someone is taken away. For example, the loss of health or financial stability, a divorce or termination of a long-term relationship, the death of a spouse, a child, or parent are events that can lead to grief. These all contribute to the emotion of grief. It is commonly believed today that there are five stages to grief.

The five stages of grief are:

- Denial: (This is not happening to me!)
- Anger: (Who can I blame and why is this happening to me)
- Bargaining: (I promise I will be a better person if . . .)
- Depression: (I can't do anything, I am too sad, and I don't care anymore)
- Acceptance: (I can deal with and I am ready for whatever comes)

Nevertheless, whatever stage one may be in during the grieving process, God knows. Because He knows our sorrow, He knows our pain, and He wants us to come through this process better and not bitter.

Hannah was a woman who was grieved and over the years had become bitter. Hannah became so heavy with bitterness she could no longer carry it so she prayed to God. The Bible tells us in 1 Samuel 1:1-28, that Hannah was married to Elkanah who had two wives Peninnah and Hannah. Peninnah had children and Hannah had no children. Every year, Elkanah went up to the City of Shiloh to sacrifice to the Lord of hosts.

And when the time was that Elkanah offered, he gave to Peninnah his wife, and to all her sons and her daughters, portions but unto Hannah he gave a worthy portion; for he loved Hannah: but the Lord had shut up her womb (1 Samuel 1:4-5).

Elkanah gave a worthy, or rather much larger, portion to Hannah than he did to Peninnah because he really loved Hannah. The New International Version puts it this way: "he gave a double portion" to Hannah. Unfortunately, Hannah had another desire than the things her husband could provide for her. She had his love and she had his wealth, but she still had a deep-seated longing to have his child. This is a great example of money not being able to buy happiness. You can have millions of dollars in the bank, but if you are unable to get what your heart desire, you can become grieved at heart. When we do not have that which we desire, only God's spirit of peace and joy can give us rest and contentment. To add to Hannah's troubles, Elkanah's second wife, Peninnah provoked Hannah deliberately for years to irritate her. Peninnah made Hannah cry often times causing Hannah to lose her appetite.

> And her adversary also provoked her sore, for to make her fret, because the Lord had shut up her womb. . . . so year by year, when she went up to the house of the Lord, so she provoked her therefore she wept, and did not eat (1 Samuel 1 6-7).

The New International Reader's Version puts it this way

> Peninnah teased Hannah to make her angry. She did it because the Lord had kept Hannah from having children. Peninnah teased Hannah year after year. Every time Hannah would go up to the house of the Lord, Elkanah's other wife would tease her. She would keep doing it until Hannah cried and wouldn't eat (1 Samuel 6-7).

What kind of feelings could Hannah have harbored in her heart during her years of barrenness?

Hannah may have had feelings of jealousy toward Peninnah because of the children Peninnah bore. There may have also been feelings of self-worthlessness or resentment toward God because of her inability to conceive a child. Additionally, Hannah may have felt like a failure because she was childless in a society that considered barrenness the ultimate failure. It is unfortunate today that many young girls believe that they can have sex before marriage and then kill their babies by aborting them. This does not please God. There is no reason why a child should be aborted except extenuating circumstances or it causes great danger to the mother's health. The truth is no child God gives to us is an accident, and that there is a purpose for each of us on Earth. The enemy has found a way to kill God's apostles, prophets, evangelists, pastors, and teachers before they are born. God is grieved with our nations stance on aborting unwanted children. We must stop! As we continue to examine the life of Hannah, we see the feelings she harbored in her heart had increased over the years.

These feelings increased to such a degree that Hannah is unable to eat or keep the tears from falling from her eyes. Her husband loved her and cared about how she felt because when he saw her crying and not eating, he asked:

> Hannah, why weepest thou? And why eatest thou not? And why
> is thy heart grieved? Am not I better to thee than ten sons? (1
> Samuel 1:8)

He saw that she was grieved at heart because of her actions. This is an example of negative emotions manifesting in your body bringing out negative words and actions. I have heard many pastors say, our thoughts have emotions associated with them. All thoughts are emotionally charged, so when you bring a thought up into consciousness, you also bring up the attached emotion. It is believed by many today that thoughts and emotions are a cause of many of the sicknesses and illnesses in the body. Hannah was beginning to show how she felt about not being able to give her husband a baby. Her grief was so deep-seated that her mourning became public. Hannah was no longer able to hide her feelings. How long Hannah grieved over her situation, the Bible does not say; but what it does tell us is that she had become bitter in her soul because we read, after the family finished eating and drinking:

> And she was in bitterness of soul, and prayed unto the Lord,
> and wept sore. And she vowed a vow, and said, O Lord of hosts,
> if thou wilt indeed look on the affliction of thine handmaid,
> and remember me, and not forget thine handmaid, but wilt
> give unto thine handmaid a man child, then I will give him
> unto the Lord all the days of his life, and there shall no razor
> come upon his head. (10-11).

Here we read Hannah crying and praying in bitterness of soul. If you find yourself bitter in your soul over situations that have happened in your life, you must pray. One way of being free from toxic emotions, feelings, and thoughts is prayer. Do not allow them to harbor in your heart for years. They will ultimately do damage to the body. Forgive and repent from the bitterness, toxic feelings, and negative emotions. For years Hannah must have waited not really accepting her barrenness, we see her denial turn into anger, bitterness, and depression; Hannah comes to the end of her strength and her own abilities and begins to bargain with the Lord. She vows a vow that, if the Lord gives her a son, she will give him back to the Lord. Hannah desperately wanted a child and in absolute surrender to her situation she remembers the Law of Moses and the Vow of the Nazarite. Hannah knew what she was asking.

> And the LORD spake unto Moses, saying: Speak unto the
> children of Israel, and say unto them, When either man or

woman shall separate themselves to vow a vow of a Nazarite . . .
He shall separate himself from wine and strong drink . . . he
shall be holy . . . All the days of his separation he is holy unto
the LORD (Numbers 6).

A Nazarite vow is usually for 30, 60 or 90 days, but Hannah vowed to
give the child up for the rest of his life. You may have had to give your
child up, and you are suffering with grief; turn it over to the Lord, and
ask him for His peace. God loves you so much, and He desires for your
life to be full of joy, but you must be willing to let the mistakes of your
past go. Hannah knew that her child would not be at many, if not all, of
the family functions. She knew he would not be able to shave his hair.
She also knew he would not be able to attend any of the family funerals,
not even hers. However, in her pain, anguish, and grief she was now able
to surrender to the Lord and vow a solemn vow. Hannah was provoked
to pray; and the Bible says, while she was talking to the Lord, one of the
priests in the Temple, Eli, saw Hannah moving her mouth as she spoke
from her heart. Eli thought she was drunk. When Eli questioned her
about it and told her to 'put away thy wine from thee, Hannah said,

No, my lord, I am a woman of a sorrowful spirit: I have drunk
neither wine nor strong drink, but have poured out my soul before the
Lord . . . for out of the abundance of my complaint and **grief** have I
spoken . . . (15-16).

Then Eli answered and said, "go in peace: and the God of Israel grant
thee thy petition that thou hast asked of him." We then read that Hannah
"went her way, and did eat, and her countenance was no more sad."
After Hannah's encounter with the man of God her attitude changed
before her condition did. She had a greater hope and the peace of God
(1 Samuel 1:18). Being in the presence of God and around the people of
God who will encourage you always bring hope, peace and contentment.
Contentment comes with believing God and finding rest in him. And
the Bible says it came to pass, "Hannah conceived and bore a son and
called his name Samuel and she lent him to the Lord all the days of his
life" (1 Samuel 1:20-28). Hannah's grieving and mourning had come to
an end. Her hopes, dreams, and desires, although she thought had died
in her past, were now in her future. After keeping her vow to the Lord,
Hannah gave the child to the Lord. And the Lord gave Hannah seven
more children and Hannah praised and exalted God (1 Samuel 2:1).

Hannah's trust was now totally in God. I believe Hannah had to renew her mind and yield to God because of her heart issues. She did this by remembering God's word, praying, seeking forgiveness, and then making her request known unto God. Hannah was a woman of great beauty. So her trust may have been in her flesh, the outward person of Hannah. As the years went by, however, she obviously knew her beauty was fading. How frightened she must have been because what she trusted in was slipping away. There are many women today who trust in their beauty just like Hannah. These women are on the road leading to disappointment, despair, and discouragement. There are many others who believe they do not look good enough and are grieving because they do not look like the models they see on television or in magazines. They are unable to look picture perfect. This is a way for the enemy to distract them and make them feel less than who they really are and that is a child of the Most High God. God says of His children, I knew you in your mother's belly and I formed you (Psalm 29:9-10; Jeremiah 1:5). He says you are wonderfully made (Psalm 149:14). Love who you are, child of God, and embrace your inner beauty by feeding your inner spirit the word of God. This will give you an inner quality and a strength that will last for the rest of your life.

Another thought to consider is that Hannah may have put her trust in her position as being the first wife to Elkanah and having his love. She knew her husband loved her and favored her over his other wife because he told and showed her. But she would find out that trusting in the position she has would fail to fulfill her deep-seated need. Dear reader, are you a person who is puffed-up because of the position you have on your job, in your church, or in your group? Pride and haughtiness are not pleasing to God. The Bible says that "pride goes before destruction, a haughty spirit before a fall" (Proverbs 16:18). Unfortunately, the person of Hannah, nor the position of Hannah, would be able to fulfill her longing to have a child. It is not until she came to the Lord with a sorrowful and repentant heart that her request was made known to God and her prayer was answered. Hannah's grieving turned into bitterness but her bitterness and grieving, after putting her faith in God, ultimately turned into joy. Do you need joy today? Do you want the pain in your grieving heart to turn into joy? Then cast all your cares on Him because He does care for you (1 Peter 5:7). You must be willing to repent and have faith in God.

Another Biblical character who was grieved in his heart was Nehemiah. Nehemiah was a man grieved to action. Nehemiah was the king's cupbearer and his ancestors resided in Jerusalem before he begin his service in Persia (Nehemiah 1:11—2:3). While Nehemiah was in "Shushan the palace," one of his brothers came to him with other men of Judah and gave him disturbing news about Jerusalem and the Jews who had escaped. The men told Nehemiah the following:

> The remnants that are left of the captivity there in the province
> are in great affliction and reproach; the wall of Jerusalem also
> is broken down, and the gates thereof are burned with fire.
> (Nehemiah 1:3)

Nehemiah records when he heard these words, "I sat down and wept, and mourned certain days, and fasted, and prayed before the God of heaven" (1:4).

Dear friend, is there anything broken in your life that is in need of repair such as a broken relationship, addictive behaviors, or character defects? You must be willing to pray. Nehemiah, while in captivity was a man of prayer. He was also a man who had a love and passion for the welfare of his brethren and the land of his fathers. When he heard of "the great affliction and reproach" of the people, when he heard that "the wall of Jerusalem [was] broken down," and when he heard "the gates . . . [were] burned with fire," Nehemiah became grief stricken (Nehemiah 1:3). He was so stricken with grief he sat down while he wept, mourned, fasted, and prayed for a number of days (Nehemiah 1:4). Nehemiah knew God because he acknowledges him as the "God of heaven." Also, Nehemiah acknowledges some of the Lord's attributes saying:

I beseech thee, O Lord God of heaven, the great and terrible God that keepeth covenant and mercy for them that love him and observe his commandments.

In my previous book, *"10 Things God Expects,"* I pointed out the prophets and patriarchs of old acknowledged God's dwelling place in heaven; for example, Moses (Deuteronomy 4:39), Solomon (11 Chronicles 6:21), and David (Psalm 11:4) all began by acknowledging this truth. Even Jesus told his disciples to pray to God the Father who art in heaven, now we read Nehemiah leading his prayer and acknowledging God as the God of heaven. Nehemiah also points out that God is great, He is terrible, He is a covenant keeper, and He is merciful to those who love him. As he continues to pray, then Nehemiah makes a request and points out Israel's sins saying:

> Let thine ear now be attentive, and thine eyes open, that thou mayest hear the prayer of thy servant, which I pray before thee now, day and night, for the children of Israel thy servants, and confess the sins of the children of Israel, which we have sinned against thee; both I and my father's house have sinned. (Nehemiah1:6)

Nehemiah shows great humility by requesting God to hear his prayer. You can almost feel Nehemiah's heart in his prayer. Nehemiah recognizes he is God's servant and he is humbly requesting his attention. He then admits he is a sinner and that he and the house of Israel have sinned against the Lord. It is so important for us to confess our sins to the Lord when we go to him in prayer. God loves it when we are truthful with him. He said, "when we confess, that which we know is wrong and sinful, He will forgive us and cleanse us for those sins" (1 John 1:9).

> We have dealt very corruptly against thee, and have not kept the commandments, nor the statutes, nor the judgments, which thou commanded thy servant Moses. (Nehemiah 1:7)

Nehemiah points out that Israel has broken every one of the commandments of God, and has not kept His statutes or judgments that were written by Moses. Nehemiah then gets honest with God about the sins committed by Israel. Instead of "they," Nehemiah says "we" identifying himself with his brethren. He then brings to God's remembrance the promises that God gave Moses saying:

> Remember, I beseech thee, the word that thou commanded thy servant Moses, saying, if ye transgress, I will scatter you abroad among the nations: But if ye turn unto me, and keep my commandments, and do them; though there were of you cast out unto the uttermost part of the heaven, yet will I gather them from thence, and will bring them unto the place that I have chosen to set my name there (Nehemiah 1:8-9).

God loves it when we bring His word to His remembrance. He said, "Come let us reason together" (Isaiah 1:18). *The Message* interpretation of the Bible puts it in today's vernacular and gives a clearer view of what Nehemiah is saying to the Lord: "We haven't done what you told us,

haven't followed your commands, and haven't respected the decisions
you gave to Moses your servant. All the same, remember the warning you
posted to your servant Moses: 'If you betray me, I'll scatter you to the four
winds, but if you come back to me and do what I tell you I'll gather up
all these scattered peoples from wherever they ended up and put them
back in the place I chose to mark with my Name'" (Nehemiah 1:7-9).
Nehemiah is recalling all that was said to Moses and reminding God, "you
are not a man that you should lie, nor the son of man that you should
repent . . ." (Numbers 23:14). Listen how Nehemiah acknowledges what
God said and what the people of God did.

> Now these are thy servants and thy people, whom thou hast
> redeemed by thy great power, and by thy strong hand.

Nehemiah now reminds the Lord what He has done in the past and
how He has redeemed Israel before and "established a testimony in
Jacob, and appointed a law in Israel (Psalm 78:5). He is reminding the
Lord of the great power He used when, "He divided the sea, and caused
them to pass through; and he made the waters to stand as an heap"
(Psalm 78:13). Nehemiah is reminding the Lord about the strong hand
he used when His remnant was in the wilderness and "in the daytime . . .
[how] he led them with a cloud, and all the night with a light of fire."
Nehemiah reminds God it was He who "clave the rocks in the wilderness,
and gave them drink as out of the great depths" (Psalm 78:14-15) And
then, "He brought streams also out of the rock, and caused waters to
run down like rivers" (Psalm 78:16). Nehemiah stated, God you were the
one who "commanded the clouds from above, and opened the doors of
heaven, and had rained down manna upon them to eat, and had given
them of the corn of heaven. Man did eat angel's food: he sent them meat
to the full" (Psalm 78:23-25). Nehemiah said, "God they were a rebellious
people who did not trust you but ye provided for them anyhow and now,
Lord God," Nehemiah is pleading, "I need you to hear me and help me."
The Scriptures record the following:

> O Lord, I beseech thee, let now thine ear be attentive to the
> prayer of thy servant, and to the prayer of thy servants, who
> desire to fear thy name: and prosper, I pray thee, thy servant this
> day and grant him mercy in the sight of this man . . . (1:11).

Nehemiah wanted the Lord to hear his prayer. Nehemiah is also
interceding on behalf of God's people. He tells God, your people want to
prosper and desire to reverence you. Nehemiah prayed and was grieved

at what he heard and wanted to make a difference in his country and ease the suffering of the people of God; and God granted Nehemiah his prayers. Today God is waiting on individuals to be grieved at heart and moved to action to ease the suffering of hurting and helpless people around the world. There are men and women in the body of Christ who are grieved in their heart like Nehemiah and Hannah. Some are grieved to action and some are grieved to bitterness yet both need the Lord for His strength and both need the Lord to see change.

Nehemiah was a man that loved his country and his countrymen and became grieved and moved to action. Hannah was grieved to bitterness. A woman that appeared to love self and was focused on her needs and her desires alone until she opened her heart to the Lord. There are many that are grieved in their spirit today because of the loss of something or someone, it maybe you reader! Nevertheless, I want you to know that grief is an emotion that can destroy your life or change your life for the better. It all depends on you. If you desire a better future for you and others, you can pray and repent and ask God to give you the strength to be moved to action. Or, you can become bitter over your loss. If you are grieved in heart and seek a change of heart, it is time for you to repent!

Chapter Nine

A BROKEN HEART

The Lord is nigh unto them that are of a broken heart . . .
Psalm 34:18

At the time of this writing, Port-au-Prince, Haiti recently suffered an earthquake that measured 7.0 magnitude on the Richter Scale, on Tuesday January 12, 2010. It was the worst in the country's history. On March 11, 2011, before publication of this book, Japan was faced with even bigger disasters. Japan experienced fires as a result of an earthquake that measured 9.0 which caused a tsunami and then a nuclear catastrophe, and took the lives of more than 10,000 people within an hour. In Port-au-Prince, Haiti and Japan we have seen television images where the grounds opened up like the mouth of a killer whale. In Japan we saw the waters rush in from the sea washing away normalcy in a matter of seconds for millions. The images portrayed on television and the Internet were devastating. In Port-au-Prince, there was a news video shown with cars, trucks, and houses that looked like toys quivering and tumbling on the street while the earth shook. Suddenly buildings collapsed in the middle of the day while people were working, while schools were in session, and while businesses were operating. The scenes were shocking. As the world sat and watched in horror we saw mothers crying for their young children who were in daycare, father's laying crushed to death by the sudden collapse of already poorly constructed buildings, elderly women dazed and shocked over the devastation, and confused teens and young adults uncertain of what would happen next. Dead bodies of men, women, and children were everywhere. Haitians in the USA expressed their concerns to the news media for their loved ones back home. Many governments and organizations worldwide rushed in to assist in any way they could. There were shattered dreams and broken hearts that ultimately turned into devastating nightmares. Although we as a people are often divided by nations, race, and gender, our hearts broke to see such devastation. As we see and hear these things happening, we are reminded of words from the Psalmist: "The LORD is nigh unto them that are of a broken heart . . ." (Psalm 34:18).

A heart can be broken for many different reasons: the death of a loved one, the end of a marriage, an unjust act from someone you trusted, and the loss of a dream. Also, we suffer with broken hearts from national and international events we see and hear in the news such as: millions of aborted babies, child slave trade and the suffering of people living in oppressed nations. Regardless of the reason for a broken heart, it may cause us to respond in abnormal ways. In this chapter, we will look at Biblical characters and others whose hearts were broken and how they responded. We will also investigate how God wants us to respond when we experience a broken heart.

In the Bible, Jacob was one of the Patriarchs. His name was changed to Israel by God (Genesis 32:28). He experienced a broken heart when he thought his favorite son Joseph was dead. Jacob was grieved to the point that he just wanted to die. But before I discuss his broken heart, let me give a little background on Jacob. He is the grandson of Abraham and Sarah and the son of Isaac and Rebecca. At birth, because he grabbed the heel of his twin brother, his parents named him Jacob in Hebrew meaning "heel" or "leg puller." As he grew up, he was much different than his brother Esau, who was a "cunning hunter" (Genesis 25:27). Jacob stayed at home among the tents. He was more of a momma's boy, in fact, the Bible tells us that he was loved more by his mother and that his father loved Esau more (Genesis 25:28). Because Esau was his father's favorite, Jacob must have felt that he was in the shadow of his brother. Perhaps he thought his father loved Esau more, because he was the oldest. It may have been he wished he was the oldest because his brother received more praise and more attention from his father. Despite the reason, he manipulated his brother, obtained his brother's birthright and ultimately stole his brother's blessings.

One day Jacob was cooking stew, and Esau came in from the field starved; Esau said to Jacob, "Give me some of the red stew . . . I'm starved!" (Genesis 25:29-30, The Message).

This was probably not the first time Esau came home from the field hungry. And it was probably not the first time the two traded. This trade was different. This trade was for a position rather than a something. Jacob said, "Make me a trade: my stew for your rights as first born" (Genesis 25:31). Esau may not have taken this trade-off seriously, and even if he did, he said: "I'm starving! What good is a birth right if I'm dead" (Genesis 25:32). Although Esau may not have been serious, Jacob was because he then says: "First swear to me." And Esau did. On an oath Esau traded away his rights as first born.

Did the boys know what the meaning of being the first born male in the family meant? More than likely, their father Isaac told them. Both father and grandfather no doubt shared, with the twins, the encounter they had with God.

> And the LORD appeared unto him, and said, Go not down into Egypt; dwell in the land which I shall tell thee of: Sojourn in this land, and I will be with thee, and will bless thee; for unto thee, and unto thy seed, I will give all these countries, and I will perform the oath which I sware unto Abraham thy father; And I will make thy seed to multiply as the stars of heaven, and will give unto thy seed all these countries; and in thy seed shall all the nations of the earth be blessed; Because that Abraham obeyed my voice, and kept my charge, my commandments, my statutes, and my laws (Genesis 26:2-5).

So not only did they understand the meaning of the first born male and its blessings, they also understood that to swear a thing out of your mouth is like a law written on paper. Jacob now owned the birthright in the spiritual realm, but now he needed it in the physical realm. After Esau had sworn his birthright away to Jacob, Jacob undoubtedly mentions this to his mother. Maybe even his father. His dad may not have thought anything of the trade because he believed the real blessing came through his words, and he knew the blessing would go to Esau. But Jacob's mother when she was told, probably thought back when she was pregnant with the twins, and inquired of the Lord why the children struggled within her belly. I am sure Jacob's mother kept the words close in her heart when the Lord told her: "Two nations are in thy womb, and two manner of people shall be separated from thy bowels; and the one people shall be stronger than the other people; and the elder shall serve the younger" (Genesis 25:23). When Jacob told his mother about getting Esau's birthright, she, at that point, probably understood more of the prophecy. So "when Isaac was old and his eyes dim," she heard her husband tell Esau to hunt for "venison" so that they would eat and he would then bless him. It was at that point, that Rebecca devised a plan for Jacob to receive the blessing from his father (Genesis 27). Rebecca told her younger son to "fetch two goats from their flock so she could cook them for her husband. Then she took Esau clothes and told Isaac to put them on, and took the skin of the goats and wrapped them around his arms and neck. When Jacob entered the room, he sat with his father and his father blessed him. When Esau came back home and cooked the meat for his father, he took it in only to find out what his brother had done. This left Esau with a broken heart; his broken heart led him to plot his brother's murder (Genesis 27:41-46).

There are many people who have killed because of a broken heart. And like Esau, they plot to kill because of a heart that had been broken. Being fired from a job, molestation or kidnapping a child, a lie that damaged a reputation, and, stolen treasures can all leave you with a broken heart. Feelings of hopelessness and helplessness can leave you in a state of confusion and rage. You can become devastated and want to destroy those who have left you feeling enraged and angry. But the Bible instructs us to love our enemies (Matthew 5:44). We are to do good to them that intentionally harm us and pray for them who despitefully use us. Perhaps prayer is what Esau did. Or perhaps the passing of time healed his broken heart. Or maybe both. Whatever the case, we see Esau with a more loving and forgiving heart toward his brother (Genesis 33:8-16)

As we look at time unfolding in the life of Jacob, we now see him as a father of twelve with plenty of goods, menservants, maidservants, two wives, their handmaidens, and twelve sons, "Jacob loved his son Joseph more than all his other sons because he was the son of his old age" and Joseph was the first born of Rebecca the wife whom he loved (Genesis 37:3). Joseph's brothers hated him because he would tell their father all they had done. Because Joseph was his dad's favorite son, Jacob made Joseph a "coat of many colors." Joseph was also a dreamer who would dream dreams and told his brothers of his dreams and they hated him even more. One day Jacob sent Joseph out to see if all was well with his older brothers. Jacob wanted Joseph to bring back a report on what the others were doing. When Joseph met up with his brothers, they wanted to kill him; instead, they sold him to a band of Medianite merchants. They then took the coat back to their father and when he recognized the coat he said, "It's my son's coat; an evil beast hath devoured him; Joseph is without doubt rent in pieces" (Genesis 37:33). Two things I want you to see here. First, Jacob had several encounters with the Lord, so he knew God was with him at some level. God protected him, provided for him, and favored him. So why, in the face of tragedy, would he not inquire of the Lord? I believe Jacob stop trusting in the Lord. All was well with him, his belly was full, there was plenty in his home, his children were now working, and he was in a state of complacency and contentment. I believe he stopped communing with God which led to a lack of trust in God. **Child of God, when the Lord blesses you with plenty, it is a time to seek him more. Learn more of who he is and what he desires because during times of trouble, you know He is with you. You know that He will be your compass and your Guide through the valley. There are times when you are in His presence, the Lord will tell of those things to come. He will prepare you for troubled times.** Jacob was unprepared for this tragedy. He believed that his son was dead. Jacob "rent his clothes, and put sackcloth upon his loins, and mourned for his son many days (Genesis 37:34). The Bible says his sons and all his daughters tried to comfort him "but he refused to be comforted; saying: 'For I will go down into the grave unto my son mourning' thus his sons wept for him." The pain of losing the one son he loved the most, his favorite child left Jacob with a broken heart and wanting and waiting to die. His broken heart left him with such strong feelings of depression that he said he would carry to his grave. Later in Genesis we see father and son reunite. I am sure Jacob stopped to thank God for seeing his son again. I am sure he was delighted because his mourning turned into joy and his tragedy became triumphant. Child of God, you must be willing to seek Jesus before and especially during times of tragedy. God wants a relationship with you. He wants to be a part of your life, and if you are hurting or your heart is broken He can and will heal you. He is a repairer of the breach and He is able to mend a broken heart. He can and will put the pieces back together again; all you need do is repent.

Before my ex-husband and I decided to have our third child, we went everywhere together. During the pregnancy, I stopped hanging out, and my ex-husband began hanging out with friends on his job. Some were women who I did not know. Before long, he was hanging out most of the time and he started receiving phone calls when he was home. I found notes left in his pants from women and lipstick on his collars, passion marks on his neck and scratches on his back.

I wanted to believe he was faithful at first, but the more I trusted in him, the less interested he seemed in my feelings. It seemed as if my world was crumbling down all around me. I began to inflict injuries on my body in an attempt to gain his sympathy and attention. I worried so much that I was hospitalized with an ulcer while I was pregnant. My world, my life, and my heart were broken into little pieces and, I believed destroyed forever. All the storybooks taught me that a man and a woman got married, had children, and they lived happily ever after. Shockingly and suddenly, I had entered into reality and was thrust out of the fairy tale world. When our son was born, I had lost all respect for my husband and just wanted life to end because I wanted the pain to end. I tried a couple of suicide attempts and drugs, alcohol, and fast living became my refuge, but they kept me in misery and darkness. As I was sinking deeper into the abyss of darkness, I heard about a man who loved me so much that He died for me. I called on Him and my Lord Jesus pulled me out of darkness and brought me into His marvelous light. Jesus showed me the way to our heavenly Father. He then gave me His precious Holy Spirit to help me live victoriously in this earthen vessel. Oh my friends, how grateful I am for God's grace and mercy. How thankful I am for His goodness and His calling. He placed his hand upon my life and then bought me out of a self-destructive life style. My life has never been the same after I repented. Glory to God!

As you have seen from these accounts, a broken heart can lead to utter depression and despair, attempted suicide, and attempted homicide. Whenever a heart has been broken, it will seem as if life will never be the same. And in some ways it will not but it can be better. A new normal begins, and in some cases, it is better than the old one. Take God's servant Job, for example, who lost everything. Job was a man of great wealth. He lost his business, his money, his children, his wife, and most of his friends. In the end, Job regained all that he lost and more. You may find yourself bitter after a broken heart, but it will get better. You may be full of rage right now, but you can be full of joy. You may be depressed right now because of your circumstances, but you can have God's peace. The Bible says "weeping may endure for a night, but joy comes in the morning" (Psalm 30:5). How does joy come? By taking it one day at a time and trusting God to bring you through the dark moments of your life. The Lord is nigh unto them that are of a broken heart. When your heart is broken and it appears that things are impossible, the

Lord is near and it then becomes his opportunity to show up. So do not give up. Keep praying, fasting and reading His word. Keep believing His word because He will do what He promised.

Forgiveness is a huge part of winning the battle and having victory over your situation and circumstances as well. Jesus said when you pray, say ". . . forgive us our debts as we forgive our debtors" (Matthew 6:12). He further admonished "And when ye stand praying, forgive, if ye ought against any: that your Father also which is in heaven may forgive you your trespasses. But if ye do not forgive, neither will your Father which is in heaven forgive your trespasses" (Mark 11:25). And he instructed us as follows, "Judge not, and ye shall not be judged; condemn not and ye shall not be condemned; forgive and ye shall be forgiven" (Luke 6:37). You may be saying but you do not know what she did to me. Or, I will never forgive her for what she has done to my child. You are right I may not know or understand but God does. He knows the hurt, pain, frustration, and anguish that you had or are experiencing right now. God wants you to give it to Him. In the Bible, He beckons us "Come unto me all ye that labor and are heavily laden and I will give you rest" (Matthew 11:28). God wants you to rest in his love, His peace, and His joy. He wants you to have faith in Him believing that He can turn your scars into stars. God wants you to know if you give him those murderous thoughts, if you give him those thoughts of suicide, and if you give him the thoughts of despair and anguish and repent, he can and will heal you. If you repent and ask forgiveness for the rage and frustration he will give you his peace. If you, dear sinner, ask God to take the broken pieces of your heart and the shattered pieces of your life and put it back together, He will. All He asks you to do is turn from those sinful thoughts and sinful ways and repent.

Chapter Ten

A REPENTANT HEART

THEREFORE SAY UNTO THE HOUSE OF ISRAEL, THUS SAITH THE LORD GOD; REPENT, AND TURN YOURSELVES FROM YOUR IDOLS; AND TURN AWAY YOUR FACES FROM ALL YOUR ABOMINATIONS
(Ezekiel 14:6)

It is essential for every believer to understand that in order to receive supernatural gifts from God; you must be in a relationship with God at a depth where it is intimate and personal. In order to have an intimate and personal relationship with God, you must spend time with Him. Not a mere five minutes, or once a day, or when you are in weekly Sunday service. No, God wants us to spend time with him throughout the day, every day. Further, in order for God to spend time with us, we must be in right standing with Him. In order for us to be in right standing with Him, we must repent of our sins. Repentance must take place in order to enter into God's kingdom (Tucker, 2009).

Repentance is very important. The reason why we know it is important is because John the Baptist taught it (Matthew 3:2), Jesus also taught it (Matthew 4:17), and Paul wrote about it saying, "God commands it." While addressing the men of Athens in his eloquent Mar's Hill speech,

Paul said, "For as much then as we are the offspring of God, we ought not to think that the Godhead is like unto gold, or silver, or stone, graven by art and man's device. And the times of this ignorance, God winked at; but now **commanded all men everywhere to repent**" (Acts 17:29-30). In other words, God was not made by the hands of men and will no longer accept this ignorance from man. Repentance from sin and dead works is what God requires, and it is essential in order to enter into His kingdom. As we covered earlier in this text, repent means to turn away from, leave alone, or change course of direction. It ". . . involves a change for the better, an amendment. Hence, it signifies to change one's mind or purpose" (Vines, p. 280). The Lord makes it plain that He wants His children to repent. He told the Israelites: "Therefore I will judge you, O house of Israel, every one according to his ways, saith the Lord God. Repent, and turn yourselves from all your transgressions; so iniquity shall not be your ruin" (Ezekiel 18:30).

The book of Ezekiel records how God gave the children of Israel the gift of fame and fortune. Eventually, they forgot it was of God, and they began relying on themselves and their gifts and talents. They believed that their health and material wealth was God's approval of their spiritually corrupt lives, their immorality, and their theological error and propensity to worship other gods. In Ezekiel 14:6, the Lord told the prophet, Ezekiel, "Say unto the house of Israel, Thus saith the Lord God; Repent, and turn yourselves from your **idols** . . ." What might be our idols today? Masses of people idolize singers, actors, sports stars, and other people. Other people are found idolizing things such as name brand clothing, shoes, furniture, homes, and cars. Additionally, we see people idolizing jewelry, art, autos, businesses, and even ministries. This is a deplorable situation with God's people. Unfortunately, with many people today, the focus is on things made by man's hands; consequently, this is the same error the people of Israel encountered and embraced. It is presently clear that the hearts of men are turned away from God and are now "serving the creation rather than the creator" (Romans 1:25). God is forgiving and merciful. He is waiting for His children to repent. God also tells His children in Ezekiel 14:6: "Turn away your faces from all your **abominations**." The Hebrew word abomination means "something disgusting." In the book of Ezekiel, the word is written over twenty-five times. In chapter sixteen, the Bible mentions what is truly disgusting to the Lord. Please take a few minutes and read Ezekiel Chapter 16:15-34, and compare it with the works of the flesh Paul talks about in Galatians 5:19-21. The Bible states that anyone doing such works cannot enter the kingdom of heaven. Now, if we want to enter into the kingdom of heaven, we must repent from idolatry and abominations. We must repent from doing the works of the flesh and idolizing the works of man's hands. We must repent for our disbelief and disobedience of God's commandments. Walking contrary to the commandments of God will keep us from entering into his kingdom. The following is a list that will hinder us from entering into the kingdom of God:

> Hate, rage, lack of self-control, murder, witchcraft, and casting spells, demon worship, backbiting, lying, boastfulness, arrogance, haughtiness, jealousy, envy, pride, fear, doubt, unbelief, slothfulness, laziness, unforgiveness, addictions, gambling, impatience, theft, lack of respect for authority, all manner of sexual sin, homosexuality, rape, pornography, group sex, child molestation, wrath, strife, reveling, pride, plotting evil and the like.

These are things God hates and these will hinder you from inheriting that which God has for you in His kingdom (Proverbs 6:16-19). Today, if you are entangled with anyone of these things and your desire is to break free and enter into the kingdom of God, repent! Make a conscientious decision that you will turn away from sin, and change the course of your life by changing the attitude and behaviors that are abominations to God. Now, today is the day to repent and ask God to forgive you by saying the prayer of repentance I have on the next page. Repent, dear child of God repent!

Conclusion

Dear Reader:

I leave you with this prayer of repentance. If there is anything in your thoughts, actions, words and deeds that may be hindering you from allowing God's spirit to live and dwell in your heart, then pray this prayer of repentance. Pray with a heartfelt sorrow to the Lord accepting God's son Jesus into your heart and allowing His Holy Spirit to begin to lead, guide and order your footsteps. God Bless You

Prayer of Repentance

Father God, in the name of your Son Jesus, I confess to you today that I have sinned against you. At times, I have even sinned against you knowingly and willingly. I pray today you forgive me of my sins. Lord, today I repent by turning away from my sinful lifestyle. I turn away and give my life to you Lord. I repent today and turn from all sinful ways and actions. I repent today and turn from idols, I repent today and turn away from abominations, and I ask that you forgive me of these things. I open up the door of my heart and allow you to come in and live in me and through me. So from this moment on, I believe the gospel and I denounce all things that displease you and oppose your Word. I do this so that I may have access to your kingdom here on earth and live in eternity with you. I thank you heavenly Father for forgiving me. I pray that you take my life, clean me up, and allow me to be a vessel of use for you. Today is the day I turn from sin and repent.